A TEXAN IN ENGLAND

Books by J. Frank Dobie

A VAQUERO OF THE BRUSH COUNTRY

CORONADO'S CHILDREN

ON THE OPEN RANGE

TONGUES OF THE MONTE

THE FLAVOR OF TEXAS

APACHE GOLD AND YAQUI SILVER

JOHN C. DUVAL:
First Texas Man of Letters

THE LONGHORNS

A TEXAN IN ENGLAND

J. Frank Dobie

A TEXAN

IN

ENGLAND

LITTLE, BROWN AND COMPANY · BOSTON

1945

Published May 1945
*Reprinted May 1945 (**twice**)*
Reprinted June 1945
*Reprinted July 1945 (**twice**)*

DEDICATION

At the English-Speaking Union in Cambridge, Mrs. Belinda Norman-Butler, as wise as she is vivacious, daily makes the lives of American and Allied soldiers, enlisted men as well as officers, more gracious. She has read most of this book in manuscript and made me aware of matters to which I had been blind. I want to dedicate it to her.

"Nothing so predisposes men to understand as making them feel that they are understood."

— GREY OF FALLODON

Acknowledgments

The author wishes to thank the following publishers for permission to quote from their authors: —

Coward-McCann, Inc., for lines reprinted by permission of Coward-McCann, Inc., publishers, from *The White Cliffs*, copyright 1940 by Alice Duer Miller.

Dodd, Mead & Company, Inc., for lines from *The Collected Poems of Rupert Brooke.* Copyright 1915 by Dodd, Mead & Company, Inc.

E. P. Dutton & Co., Inc., for an excerpt from *Book of a Naturalist* by W. H. Hudson.

J. B. Lippincott Company for lines reprinted by permission from "The Admiral's Ghost" from *Collected Poems*, Volume 2, by Alfred Noyes (copyright 1910 by J. B. Lippincott Company); and for lines reprinted with permission of J. B. Lippincott Company from "The Barrel Organ" in *Collected Poems*, Volume 1, by Alfred Noyes (copyright 1906 by Alfred Noyes).

The Macmillan Company for lines from "The Old Squire" from the *Poetical Works* of Wilfred S. Blunt.

Charles Scribner's Sons for lines from "Primrose Way" by Robert Louis Stevenson.

P for Preface

CAMBRIDGE UNIVERSITY had been go-
ing four centuries or so when one of its sons, John Harvard, died in the Massachusetts Bay Colony bequeathing
his library, half of his estate and his name to "that eldest
of the seminaries which advance learning and perpetuate
it to posterity throughout America." That was in 1638.
It was five hundred years after Chaucer wrote *The Can-
terbury Tales* and three hundred years after Shakespeare
died before Cambridge University gave English literature
equal status with Greek and Latin. She was rushing things
up a bit when in the fall of 1942 she instituted a Professor-
ship in American History.

Henry Steele Commager of Columbia University was
invited over to break the ice and blaze the trail. He stayed
a term and was asked to nominate somebody to take up
this particular white man's burden. When he conveyed the
invitation, I explained that I hadn't read the American Constitution since I was a boy and didn't understand it then.
I pointed out that my knowledge of history consisted
mainly of facts relating to the length of the horns of Longhorn steers, the music inherent in coyote howling, the
way mother rattlesnakes swallow their young, the duels
Jim Bowie fought with his knife, the friendliness of pan-
thers in fighting tigers off helpless Mexican campers, the

location of the Lost Adams Diggings, the speed of the Pacing White Mustang, the smell of coffee boiled over mesquite wood, the ferocity of devil's horses in attacking hummingbirds, the religious note in ballads about Jesse James and Sam Bass, the shade-hunting serenity and grass-chewing leisureliness of cowboys as opposed to the "tense grim tone" that Zane Grey used to and Hollywood still does give them, the habits of ghosts in guarding Spanish treasure, how Wrong Wheel Jones got his name, and what, in general, the Southwest was like before, to quote Bigfoot Wallace, "bob wire played hell with it."

Henry Commager answered that he was aware of my ignorance of genuine history, but said it wasn't necessary to know any history to teach it to the novices at Cambridge University. He said that virtually all the young men were in armed or technical services and the young women in auxiliary branches, and that whatever I got would be absolutely at my mercy. He said my job would be as elementary as teaching a hound how to suck eggs. He said I could read one of his chapters in American history right after breakfast and relay it that morning before I forgot it. What Cambridge wanted, he said, was an explainer of America who had had American mud between his toes and grass burs in his heels. He said it wouldn't make any difference whether I took up the tariff question or the chewing gum habit. I told him I didn't know anything about the tariff and never chewed gum, and was therefore only half of a typical American. I asked him if it would be all right for me to mention Texas cattle as well as Plymouth Rock chickens. He said to go ahead with the

Rio Grande and to throw in the horned frogs if I wanted to. Meantime I had a letter from my fellow Texan, Walter Webb, at Oxford, saying to make my own definition of history and come on over.

The way those fellows talked reminded me many a time later of the old cowboy song about a tenderfoot hornswoggled into riding broncs. "To hear the boss talk," the tenderfoot says in the song,

> Cowpunching was only fun —
> But the scoundrel how he lied!

The war had been my war since it began in 1939. On a September day, four years after the Germans began the murder of humanity, I left Austin, Texas, feeling that even though I was too old to fight it was something to be going in the direction of fighting men. I had long had the conviction, stronger now than ever, that despite all Good Neighbor policies — and they are good policies — the one chemical blend that America can make with other nations is with the English-speaking ones and that the decencies and amenities of civilization in general and of our own civilization in particular depend on that blend. The only essential blend between elements is chemical; physical proximity alone never blended materials chemically opposed. Perhaps, I thought, I could add my mite to making the English-speaking nations understand each other better. To understand is to forgive.

I flew over the ocean without seeing it and realized again the distinction between transportation and travel. Towards two o'clock of the afternoon of October 6, 1943,

I got out of a taxicab in front of Emmanuel College. Because this was John Harvard's college it has cultivated an especial hospitality towards American university men, and I was to live in it the year while lecturing to Cantabrigians from all the colleges. I found a lunch, kept against my late arrival, on a fine old oak table in the front room of the set of three I was to occupy. At the evening meal "in hall" I found myself alone without a gown among the gowned Fellows. When we got up and I started filling my pipe, it was made known to me that I was heading in the wrong direction. The smoking didn't come until after a toast of welcome had been recorded in the book kept in the combination room. That welcome remained consistent, and it was added to by many people of the University and the charming old city of Cambridge.

With numerous exceptions, academicians the world over are a Lady of Shalottish kind of people looking at the reflection of life in a looking glass instead of diving into the stream of life itself. Or if they do essay diving, they are apt to be splay. A majority of them distrust vitality and are "fit to live with maiden aunts and keep tame rabbits." As scholars they must concern themselves with what has been; yet they are not to be singled out as the chief maintainers of Tory strongholds. A Tory is one who is afraid of change and affects the attitude of holiness towards things as they are, because the arrangement assures special privileges for himself. The Tory's coat of arms is a setting hen. There are always Tories everywhere. They are in the exiled Polish Government; they worship themselves in the United States Senate; they manipulate actions in all sorts of ecclesiastical and educational institutions in order to embalm their own corpses with the complexion of life. Yet, witness, I stand in bareheaded salute to all genuine scholars, of all creeds and tempers. They are the preservers and fertilizers of civilization down the ages. Only a fraction of me has ever homed in academic halls; only a fraction of this book will smell of them.

I didn't originally intend to write it; on the contrary, I proposed not to add to the books on England. The addition has at least been made without malice aforethought. It has been made because experiences within myself as well as without made me want to say something. When I came to England, I continued writing the Sunday articles — on any subject interesting to me — that I have for years been supplying to four Texas newspapers. Not long before the school year ended, I wrote a lengthy article on Cambridge life for the *Saturday Evening Post*. With many additions, subtractions and changes these articles have been woven into the book.

England is Hamlet. You can make out a case for any point of view you want to take towards it. Its life would not be so rich were it not so various, complex, self-contradictory. I have not tried to "cover" anything. I wouldn't want to write a "definitive work"; that kind of book is too exhausting to the party of the first part as well as to the second. I confess to a horror of being dull. Often I remember the story of the three men who went to see the Pope.

"And how long have you been in Rome?" the Pope asked the first man.

"Three days, Your Holiness."

"Good, you have Rome to see." Then turning to the second, he asked, "And how long have you been in Rome?"

"Three weeks, Your Holiness."

"Good, you have seen Rome."

He turned to the last of the visitors.

"Your Holiness, I have been in Rome three years."

"Good. Now you know you can never see Rome."

In pages to follow appear by name and without name numerous people who have given me something for which I am debtor. W. S. Mansfield, Director of the big University Farm at Cambridge, gave me exceptional insights into farming ways and farm people. E. Welborne, Senior Tutor at Emmanuel College, has been my mentor and friend in scores of ways. If it had not been for Herbert Nicholas, loaned by Oxford to the Ministry of Information, the loveliness of the spires and gardens of Oxford would not have come to me as they did. I'll always be remembering Orchard Lea in Cheshire, where Colonel and Mrs. J. C. H. Crosland made me live so fully; Kingfield in Cumberland, where Mildred and Captain Frank Thompson-Schwab gave me the haunting cries of the lapwing and much else along with rich welcome; winsome Doreen and Cyril Whiting, who again and again made All Saints Hall in Suffolk my home.

Writing Americans in London all bless Gwyn Barker of the Ministry of Information; I bless her for helpfulness and friendship that have gone beyond getting typed sheets across the ocean. Joanna Skipsey, in the same office, has given six chapters in this book clear-eyed criticism; she is an Elizabethan of whom I am very fond. Anne Whyte has also helped to make the office of the American Division of the M.O.I. delightful to me.

Had it not been for the abiding friendliness and hospitality of the Master and Fellows of Emmanuel College, where I have lived more than a year, I should not have wanted to write this book and I could not have written it. Remembering them, I remember also the Master's Household, the Porters, Bedmakers, Waiters, Cooks, Gardeners, Clerks, Keepers of Buttery and Library, Repair Man, Errand Boy, Secretary in the Senior Tutor's office who typed what I hope somebody else will read, the two Swans and three Ducks in the Pond, one particular Pied Wagtail using the Front Court, and other personnel of my Emmanuel home.

EMMANUEL COLLEGE, CAMBRIDGE
11 o'clock Thursday morning,
October 19, 1944

Contents

Contents

A TEXAN IN ENGLAND

CHAPTER I
Professoring at Cambridge

$\mathbf{M}$Y BUSINESS at Cambridge University was to present the United States of America historically to about twenty young men and women — deferred civilians — in one class, and to about two hundred "short course" cadets of the Royal Air Force and the Royal Navy in another. The cadets interested me more as a cross section of British life; the civilians worked me harder, for they were all specializing in history. Certainly I must not have been the only individual conscious of an uneasiness within myself when I stood before them for the first time.

I

In Texas I had been used to announcing to a roomful of young barbarians that I would discourse, say, on the Age of Horse Culture and then, after introducing a "caveyard" of Spanish mustangs, proceeding to a string of yarns about spectacular rides by pony-expressmen, horse thieves, little Felix Aubrey on a thousand-dollar bet across the

eight hundred miles of the Santa Fe Trail, and other expo-
nents of the culture. Cambridge undergraduates soon gave
me to understand that while the picturesque was entirely
agreeable to them, they were faced with severe examinations on the constitutional and political phases of history.
They said that patronage of Hollywood cinemas made
it possible to understand my accents, but some of them
wondered whether their pronunciations sounded as strange
to me as mine did to them.

They wanted to get down to bedrock on the causes
of the American Revolution — and they were as open-
minded on that subject and as easy to be frank with as
any group of Americans could possibly be. I never felt
hampered otherwise than by my own ignorance. They
were strong after interpretations of the American Constitution, the powers of the Senate, the American political
system, States' rights; they insisted on a definition of the
Democratic Party as opposed to the Republican; they
yearned for an exposition of the Negro problem and hoped
for a proposal for its solution; they wanted to know about
minority rights and were a little amused over poll taxes
in some states and corporation laws in others. They asked
about the origins of jazz music and the number of wives
allowed a Mormon. They had a consuming curiosity as
to the survival of buffaloes, the fatality of rattlesnake bites,
and the birthrate among "red Indians," always so called
to distinguish them from the proper Indians of India. In
the very beginning I found that a chapter in Morison and
Commager's *Growth of the American Republic*, two chapters in Charles and Mary Beard's *Rise of American Civili-*

zation and three chapters in anybody's life of Thomas Jefferson were not sufficient fortification for a session. The bedroom was too cold to go to bed in, anyhow, and for months I boned like a freshman.

Yet I couldn't live a cloistered life. A considerable percentage of the people in Cambridge seemed to have been saving a spoonful of tea out of their monthly rations with which to brace up the new American Professor. Some don in almost every college was inviting me to hear the blessing in Latin at his "high table." The Office of War Information, attached to the American Embassy in London, began its enduring recognition of my presence in the country by asking me to make talks to civilians on Tom Paine, Causes of the Civil War, the American Constitution and related subjects. The British Army Education office in Cambridge decided it would be uplifting to their units, especially the A.T.S., to hear the native accents of a professor from Texas. The divisional branch of the Ministry of Information knew of civilian audiences thirsting for knowledge that only an American could give them. American Red Cross clubs have designs on speakers; and Youth Conferences, very popular all over England, draft Americans in and out of uniform. A club in one college wanted me to talk on American home life, a club in another college about America before and after Pearl Harbor. I long ago learned that any speaker can start out on nearly any text and work around to his one sermon.

I was soon roped into the brains trust style of passing time and information. A parent brains trust broadcasts weekly over the B.B.C. — and I failed miserably in explain-

ing over it "Why Do Americans Read Epics?" The English-Speaking Union in Cambridge runs brains trusts; the
British Council sends trusts to American camps; there are
trusts to British camps and to town halls. A trust consists
of four or five presumable possessors of brains who sit
before an audience and make a stab at answering questions.
A chairman tries to prevent fools and cranks from monopo-
lizing the time and to encourage questions that will lead
to thoughtfulness as well as to wit and information. I have
gone with Britishers to American camps to intermediate,
and to British camps to give the appearance of "authorita-
tiveness" on America.

Lots of times I have not known whether I was a professor or a public-relations officer. A civilian American in
the British Isles has during my period of residence been as
conspicuous, if recognized, as a gold tooth, or a rotten one
either, in a row of ivory. Texans in the Air Forces are as
thick as fiddlers in hell. Cambridge is one of their off-duty
targets. They soon found out I was here, and many a day
they, with a melting-pot seasoning of other gringos, have
come to my rooms like bees to a seep spring in Dead Horse
Canyon in summertime. God bless them! I have always
been glad to see them, but sometimes they have not con-
tributed very heavily to an argument on the infallibility
of the Supreme Court, or boiled with me over the way
American politicians look as pious as a Dominecker hen
while they apostrophize "Jeffersonian democracy" and
"Jacksonian democracy" without being able to give a single concrete fact about either.

There are always valid reasons for going to London.

During the winter months I would go up there often, get warm and feel myself in the throbbing world. I have never gone without eagerness or returned without reluctance. This is my first visit to England, but since I was very young I have been reading English poetry. When spring came I decided that it was utterly immoral for me to be either a professor or a public-relations agent. I wanted to boat up the Cam River with students, lie down on the lea side of a haystack and listen to the soaring skylarks, be kept awake by nightingales, hunt for lapwing eggs, smell primroses, pluck cowslips, waylay a Shropshire shepherd, be instructed by a rabbit poacher and otherwise acquire some really useful knowledge. Duty, "stern lawgiver," kept interfering.

2

The relationship between the seventeen men's and two women's colleges and the University is analogous to that between the forty-eight states and the Union; the states own most of the territory and the Union owns all the states. The colleges house students, feed them, encourage their development into high-minded citizens, employ porters to see that the door to the outside world, which is hard by the porter's lodge, is closed by ten o'clock at night, though they can ring a bell and get in free until midnight, after which they must either produce a pass or get fined, unless they crawl over the wall. The Senior Tutor of a college stands to students in the place of parents; other tutors supervise their studies. All lectures, laboratories and degrees are provided by the University.

Every college except one for women, whose founder stipulated otherwise, has a chapel, though attendance ceased to be compulsory years ago. A college dean can usually count on a more numerous congregation than the nine old men who every Sunday afternoon give ear to a bishop or some other dignitary preaching the traditional University sermon in Great Saint Mary's Church. Every college delights in its gardens, now patched with vegetables, and owns athletic grounds, considered as essential to a rounded education as the college libraries. These are replete with classics, but science and specialization have made the great University Library and various faculty (departmental) libraries essential. The absence of college politics and of many "activities," such as keeping campus newspapers going, gives collegians more time to fortify their brains.

The fare at the dons' table is often somewhat better than that the benchers below them get. The days when dons at one college had a private brewery and at another college ate and sold two or three thousand doves a year from their own dovecot passed long ago. For generations their responsibilities have been increasing and their fleshly indulgences decreasing. They have jobs, not sinecures. Potatoes are inevitable for everybody. I have always liked potatoes, but I must agree with W. H. Hudson, an Englishman who learned to eat potatoes outside of England, that the "sodden mass of flavorless starch and water," peeled before boiling, "looks like the remains of a boiled baby, boiled to a rag." I don't think that boiled asparagus looks any better, or boiled marrow, or boiled fish, or boiled carrots. I have been in constant expectation of finding the lettuce boiled. I wouldn't complain at wartime fare, only at the murder of freshness by boiling and the barbarous failure to get the taste and minerals from potato skins. Home cooking is far more civilized than the traditional cooking in some college kitchens. The British have done a grand job at feeding themselves, even if occasionally I feel like saluting young men for their ability to do on what approaches "a Spanish dinner." To eat a Spanish dinner, Grandpa used to direct, "Get down off your horse, draw up your belt a notch and get back on." I haven't drawn up my belt any notches, and it is with pride that I can echo the average Britisher, after he has called his piecrust an "Atlantic wall," "Oh well, we're not doing so bad, you know."

The dons don't do so bad when they retire from their high table to the combination (club) room and drink port and other wines — in wartime according to the depletions their ample cellars have suffered. In a few colleges snuff is offered with wine, but only in one or two that I have visited is smoking permissible before coffee arrives. To smoke before wine, thus dulling the sense of taste, is regarded not only as an exhibition of poor connoisseurship but as an affront to those with better. Wine, like the weather, is an unfailing subject for breaking silence on.

The pitch of academic conversation depends to a considerable extent on visitors from the outside world. As every college is a hostel to its own alumni and to all kinds of worldlings, a variety of talk is heard. Without visitors, it is apt to be shoppy and at times to smack of Browning's "Soliloquy of the Spanish Cloister." Only since 1882 have married men been legally admissible to fellowship in the colleges. For a man whose instincts are strong for the open and very weak for the cloistral, who has been hearty with comrades around campfires and in taverns, who has followed his own whims as to when, where, in what order he will eat, drink, smoke, be silent or open his word-hoard, there is something cramping in the daily requirement of putting on a gown at a certain minute, walking to table in ceremonious order, walking out according to rank, then sitting down for parlor relaxation in pretty much the same way, from beginning to end following a ritual. Relaxations from formulas are themselves according to rule. This is not the kind of atmosphere to make a lusty spirit jump "to put his whole wit in a jest," as if he had "resolved to live a fool the rest of his dull life."

Yet urbanity is not lacking. The system places at the head of one college an admiral; at the head of another a great lover of and authority on birds who is also a theologian; at the head of another the most popular historian of the country, who is interested in urban sanitation as well as in preserving landscapes. The author of the famous Beveridge Plan is at his Oxford home master of a college. I have certainly heard good talk in the combination room, delighted in the company, departed in fine humor with myself and everybody else. To remember some of the Fellows I have sat with will always be good medicine.

3

As for the undergraduates, in normal times fully eighty per cent of them enroll for the Honors Degree, the remainder for the Ordinary Degree. Some colleges will not admit Ordinary Degree candidates. Graduation with honors emphatically means a high standard of scholarship, which in turn means a thorough background and steady application to work. Admission is through competitive examinations, which are anything but perfunctory. Dullards and playboys simply do not get in. Every candidate's character is considered. So is his intelligence. Students are as averse to being considered grinds as American students are and are compelled to expend some energy and to exercise considerable ingenuity in seeming not to do what they do do — work. Dawdling at coffee between ten and eleven in the morning and at tea in the afternoon helps to keep up the appearance of leisureliness. Going in for cricket, rowing, rugby or some other sport helps even more, while helping also to keep a man fit for studying. In peacetime, playing the horses at Newmarket races half an hour away will give a reputation for worldliness to a rich man's son who may be essentially a hard student.

The popular idea, in their own country as well as abroad, is that all men at the two old English universities, Cambridge and Oxford, are the sons of the rich and privileged. Not half of them are from the much satirized "public schools," which are actually private. About half come from county free schools. The county system extends financial aid to promising pupils who can't get through a university without help. The old universities and colleges have been amassing endowments for centuries and can be counted on to aid financially any lad or lass of undoubted abilities who needs aid. In these war times no student has a car; in peace times, University regulations prohibit freshmen from keeping cars. I doubt if in normal times as many Cantabrigians sport as many sport cars as enliven the University of Oklahoma campus. There is probably less snobbery than at Princeton.

A strong operative for democracy is the cosmopolitan character of the student bodies at both Cambridge and Oxford. English to the backbone, these universities are anything but provincial. Every civilized country on the globe, perhaps more than one only partly civilized, is represented both in the courses offered and among the students enrolled. At a lunch given by the Vice-Chancellor of Cambridge for the Portuguese Ambassador to Great Britain, this big, dark, muscular man, who looks as if he had spent a good part of his fifty or so years indulging but not succumbing to the body's senses, replied to a toast in these words: "As an undergraduate at Cambridge, I received two things that have strongly influenced my life. I learned to respect every man's opinion. I am a devout Catholic, and I learned to tolerate every man's religion." We all felt that the Ambassador was sincere.

I thought of the reply made by an American Rhodes Scholar when asked what had struck him most forcibly about English university life. "Three thousand young men, every one of whom would rather lose a game than play it unfairly," was his reply.

The ideal of rounding out the specialist in any branch of learning is indicated by a "General Examination" that all candidates for admission to the University must take, whether they are to concentrate on Mathematics, Chemistry, Agriculture, Literature, or what. Some questions are: "What are the qualities of a good Member of Parliament?" "What meanings may be attached to the motto 'Asia for the Asiatics'?" "How may we expect science to to be applied to the lightening of household work?" "What changes in British agriculture are likely to be required after the war?" "How can people learn to appreciate good music?" "What is meant by the 'Standard of Living'?" "How far does what you have seen of the American Forces in this country confirm or modify the view of America you had already formed?" "Which do you consider the most outstanding advances in medical science since 1900?" "Do Russian novels in translation give any intelligible picture of Russia?" "What factors will determine the future status of France among the powers?"

One night just after I had come to my rooms rather late, I heard a knock at the door. I opened it with hat still on my head — where it is apt to be any time I am not sleeping. Outside in the dim light a group of undergraduates huddled and grinned. I remembered that this was the night for "bump suppers," following the boat races. One youth catapulted in, lurched back. Another stood forth.

"We want your hat," he said.

"What for?"

"To put on the flagpole."

"I'd be naked without this hat."

"You have another, haven't you?"

"No, and I could not get another like this between here and Philadelphia."

While talking I had pulled my hat off and put it on the table beside which I stood. A lad, emboldened by bump supper beer, ran in, grabbed the hat, and then away the whole crew charged, yelling "Hurrah for America!" The receding notes of a song came to my ears. I took the song to be "Where Did You Get That Hat?"

Now how I came to get that hat, 'tis very strange and funny,
Grandfather died and left me his property and money;
And when the will it was read out, they told me straight and
    flat
If I would have his money I must always wear his hat.

I had an idea that the celebrators might not stay up all night to guard my hat against the wind flirting with the flagpole. The night porter rescued it for me. I did not approve of tutorial apology for the young gentlemen the next day. If anything, the checkreins should be let out.

I had talked with some of these lads at a Saturday night debate in the undergraduate clubroom, which is provided with magazines and newspapers. The subject to be debated was: "Resolved, that the strength of an Englishman lies in his not having to think." I had myself been impressed into the argument. After we four debaters had our say, the floor opened up. Out of about twenty-five young men present, half that many volunteered speeches, nearly all of

them bent on proving that Englishmen do not think and
never have thought. Some of the ingeniousness was delicious. One cherry-faced lad made a speech that makes
me predict he will some day fill the galleries in the House
of Commons. Here was the cultivation of wits and mind-
play that in the days when the American Republic was
young made town halls and schoolhouses the best local
forums in the world. These young men were getting fun
and positive mental growth that one can't buy from the
canners of entertainment.

In another college I went to the monthly meeting of a
historical society presided over by a genial tutor. Only
about a dozen men belong to it. After coffee one of them
began reading a paper on *Punch*. As soon as he opened
his mouth there was a bolt of all other members to a case
of brown bottles I had observed in a corner of the room.
It is a part of the formalism of the society that beer shall
be drunk while the program is in progress but that nobody
shall touch beer until the speaker begins and then that
everybody shall make for it. I thought of the old cowboy
trick of asking a man to tell a story and then when he begins telling it, of dropping off into a snore. One member
of the club got a bottle of synthetic orange juice instead
of beer. Most of the men drank two or three bottles apiece
during the course of the evening. A large proportion of
University men drink beer, and think no more of it than
of drinking coffee. I have not seen any undergraduate in-
toxicated beyond gaiety.

For a costume party in one of the women's colleges, I
rented a long-tailed black coat and a wig from a local out-

fitter and introduced myself as General Sam Houston of
the Republic of Texas. General Houston met Karl Marx,
Charlotte Corday, Florence Nightingale, Henry VIII, Robert Bruce, Abraham Lincoln, and a score or so of other
characters scattered through nearly that many countries
and centuries. The disguises were about as thin as watered
milk made from milk powder. What interested me were
games calling for something creative on the part of the
players.

For the first game, the party was divided into two groups.
Each one was to decide on a historical name to act out, the
object being not to keep the other side from guessing the
name but to reveal it by skillful pantomime. It is better to
pick a name with not more than five letters. To illustrate,
my side picked NOAH. The acting out of this name consisted of five scenes. The first one was a representation of
the animals of Noah's Ark, marching around pair by pair.
The lady I was with asked me what animals we were. I
tried to bellow like a bull and she mooed like a cow. The
next four scenes, all the actors going out between each
scene, pantomimed historical characters whose names began successively with N, O, A and H. For the N we acted
out the death scene of Nelson, who, wounded to death on
his ship, was supported by Lieutenant Hardy. Nelson's last
words, in a whisper, were: "Kiss me, Hardy." As the Lord
Nelson in our act was a disguised girl, I did not mind in the
least playing the role of Hardy. For O, we acted out Oliver
Cromwell's dissolution of Parliament. ("Take that bauble
away.") For A, King Arthur sat with knights at his Round
Table. For H, Horatius held the bridge over the Tiber. No

great lover of games, I must say that the play of mind on whatever historical knowledge one may have and the spontaneous play-acting made this game delightful to me.

The traditional nonchalance of collegians is supposed to be expressed by the saying that when an Oxford man comes to Cambridge he deigns one glance and then looks as if he owned the place, whereas when a Cambridge man goes to Oxford he looks, even before he has given the place a glance, as if he didn't give a damn who owned it. Or maybe it's vice versa. Towards professors the most prideful student is polite almost to the point of deference. He inclines to be very shy until the ice is broken for him; then he may be truly companionable. In England, as on the Continent, a man of learning is supposed to be some pumpkins. No Prime Minister could be devastated by the charge that he has consulted a "long-haired" college professor. The Prime Minister's public regards knowledge as something respectable, whether long-haired, short-haired or no-haired, because the study of a great deal of evidence seems necessary for sound opinions on complicated matters. I must admit that I have felt less apologetic for my professional existence at Cambridge than I have felt in a country where two Presidents within my time have suffered grievously for not having abstained, like the sainted Harding, from all intercourse with professors.

The typical lecture room at Cambridge is provided with a kind of pulpit that would stifle any stump-speaker. It is a carpenter's Mount Sinai that leaves a Grand Canyon between the occupant and his audience. It seems designed for a clerical robe and is, indeed, reminiscent of the far past when teachers were churchmen. If I wore a gown while lecturing, I fancy I might elicit more pontifical regard from the listeners. They often cut my classes, which seems sensible. They can get any facts out of books. There is nothing like taking notes to disrupt the note-taker's attention and weaken his memory. He hears something with his physical ears and it goes out his pencil-grasping fingers, leaving his mind as blank as a gas pipe after the gas pressure is exhausted. I can tell if I interest students by noticing whether they look at me rather than at their notebooks. The dullest professors I have known have been those self-worshipers whose apparent ambition in life is to have their own words parroted back to them in examination papers. Soon after launching forth at Cambridge, however, I gave up the effort to discourage note-taking. The Cambridge rule seems to be that if you come to class you are obligated to take at least some notes to pass on to those who do not come.

As far as quality of mind is concerned — and quality of mind is something that all the theories of democracy in the world cannot equalize — there is no detectable difference between top American students and top British students. The average student at the one English University I have acquaintance with is, however, better trained mentally, has the fibers in his mind better developed, enjoys the act of thinking more and has more intellectual curiosity than the average American student. He is more civilized, just as the average member of Parliament is more civilized than the average Congressman, less given to the puerile in thought, speech and conduct. He demonstrates how the charm of youthfulness may be added to by dignity and mental maturity. He gives a richer meaning to Wordsworth's "The child is father of the man."

Go back a few years before the war to any State University in America. The first class of the morning is over. Students make a rush for breakfast or for coffee or maybe only for some form of "pep" beverage at a drugstore near at hand. Those that are not talking are looking maybe at a newspaper. What are they looking at in the newspaper? Two things generally: sports or the funnies. Within the last fifteen years a much higher percentage of American students than formerly have come to take a serious interest in political, economic, social questions. But it is still a widespread idea among American students, as well as among Americans who are not students, that amusement — entertainment — consists of something that will not require the constitutionally tired businessman to exercise his brain. The tired businessman's brain is devoted to practical things, and it isn't fun to use it. Fun is something to be bought, through a nickelodeon, in a picture show, from the voices of radio wits, out of colored Sunday supplements and their weekday counterparts.

The English collegian, on the contrary, has no colored Sunday supplement. He follows sports, goes to cinemas, wouldn't stand for having the peace of his pub or his teahouse constantly violated by jazz music; he listens to ideas as well as opiates over the radio, and reads the editorials and reports on Parliamentary debates in his newspaper. His intellectual activity is not modeled on that of the tired businessman.

4

It is human for one country or one race to build up folk-lore about other countries and races. The old frontier saying that "the only good Indian is a dead Indian" exemplifies the case — as if Indians did not differ among themselves, as well as Frenchmen. It is a part of American folklore as respects Englishmen to suppose that they are "effete." Few woolen-clad Americans who have shivered through an English winter and watched Englishmen pull up their socks over bare legs, and Englishwomen sometimes wear no socks at all, any longer entertain the idea. No human being can live in a college hall in an English University, sit in one of its living rooms, eat in its dining hall and sleep in one of its bedrooms and be remotely effete.

The architecture of these halls was designed back in the days when monks believed that the more uncomfortable man is on earth the better he will fare in heaven. The openings into the halls, on which no door ever closes, do not connect with each other; they only connect with the air. The air is no colder than the air of central Texas on a cold winter day; it is no damper than the air at the mouth of the Hudson River on a foggy night; but the peculiar chemical combination — as unanalyzable as a molecule of aroma from a cape jasmine flower on a moonlight night — is colder and more bone-chilling than the bottom of a cellar in January, is wetter than a soaked saddle blanket and more dampening than the sweat of death. This chemical combination permeates all the ancient walls of brick and stone, and to an American enduring his first December within them they are about as warming as the Great Dismal Swamp would be on the night of Doomsday.

To an American. The Englishman may and invariably does grumble at the weather, but it is only the exception who grumbles at the architecture that brings the weather in instead of shutting it out. My brain never would work unless my back was comfortable. In my college rooms I have many a day spent a good part of the forenoon poking the coal fire and backing into it before my brain would thaw out. On the other hand, I am convinced that the British collegian could sit down in a screened-in porch to an Eskimo hut built under an iceberg and study effectively. I have slept on the ground in the Rocky Mountains in zero weather, but I never felt the need of a hot-water bottle in bed until I came to Cambridge. I expect to take home my stone hot-water jug, with mouth on its side, as a souvenir. Read Shakespeare's Falstaff plays and say that the English have no sense of humor. Live in a college hall with them and then say they are effete! Effete! No wonder the English can take it.

The two women's colleges at Cambridge are regarded as architectural disharmonies. You open a door to enter one of their halls. The door closes and you find yourself in a long steam-heated corridor, on to which the rooms open. The Britisher is nearly as conservative about changing his architecture as Americans are about mending their Constitution. About a hundred and fifty years ago it was proposed to pave the main streets in Cambridge, that is, the streets among and between the colleges, and to light them better. The University people were very lukewarm on the proposals. They said that lighting the streets would increase the fighting between Town and Gown elements, as in the dark they frequently passed each other without recognition. They said that more lights would simply mean more targets for undergraduate rocks. When, much later, a new steward swept the cockroaches, root and branch, out of his college kitchen, one of the cooks asked in dismay, "What will the University Zoological Laboratory do? They have always depended on our kitchen for specimens." Before the introduction of baths from running water was halted at one college by World War I, it had been argued by the authorities that such were unnecessary; no collegian was obliged to stay in college longer than eight weeks at a time and a "saucer bath" would do him. After the American Red Cross at Cambridge took over a college hall for officers' quarters last winter, I heard the provost of the college say that he supposed it would have to be "restored" when the war is over. I asked him if restoration would include abolishment of the newly installed shower baths. He grinned no.

A Cambridge man often remarks that it would be a good thing if a great many Englishmen went to America and looked *inside* the houses there, while at the same time some Americans came to England and looked at the *outside* of houses here. I agree. It may be that by the time American citizens vote for their President directly, instead of for a passel of rubber-stamps called "electors," and by the time a minority of the Senate can no longer throttle a majority of both Congress and country, the college halls in Cambridge will have closed themselves to bitter north winds and fen damps and have warmed up their interiors. I rejoice to think they will never get so warm as a Pullman sleeper.

When one thinks on "whatsoever things are true, whatsoever things are honest, whatsoever things are just, whatsoever things are pure, whatsoever things are lovely," one must remember that these things do not reside exclusively in mechanical techniques. If they did, the superb R.A.F. radar system might be transmitting over the ether a new epic entitled "Paradise Found," Willow Run be assembling the conclusions of another Darwin, and Pittsburgh be riveting the strains of the paean of the century of the common man — who still must turn to Gray's "Elegy Written in a Country Churchyard."

Within these Cambridge walls have walked, studied, idled, laughed, shivered, dreamed, derided and left their uneradicable shadows two of the three men that Thomas Jefferson accounted the greatest the world has produced, both of them, Bacon and Newton, philosophers; Malthus with his figures on Population; Oliver Cromwell to free nations from kings, Clarkson to free slaves from owners, and Legion to free human minds; Pitt of the Parliaments and John Winthrop, "the Moses of New England"; learned Bentley and witty Walpole; Macaulay and Thackeray and then the grand roll call of poets — Spenser, Milton, Dryden, Gray, Wordsworth, Coleridge, Byron, Tennyson. No school can claim the greatest of them all, for Shakespeare belonged to the earth itself. You can see the corner in Trinity College's courtyard where Byron, forbidden to keep a dog, contemptuously chained a bear. Darwin, whose theory of evolution shook Christendom, was a Cambridge man, and Cambridge still leads the world in Physics. Walking on the "Backs," the green and quiet college gardens along the River Cam, I have recalled Emerson's hopeful assurance: "Patience, patience, with the shades of all the good and great for company."

Until about seventy-five years ago women had no chance to be numbered among the good and great of Cambridge, even though two of the greatest — perhaps the two greatest — rulers the country has had were queens. In the 'seventies some believers in feminine intelligence made it possible for a handful of young women to enter Cambridge and dine intellectually on crumbs cast from the Masters' tables. For a long time they were not admitted to men's classes but were given separate lectures in a limited number of subjects. Two women's colleges were established, well separated from the men's. After women were allowed in regular University classes, some lecturers openly flouted them. "Q" — Sir Arthur Quiller-Couch, Professor of English Literature — would always begin his lecture with the words "Young gentlemen," utterly ignoring the young ladies. Finally, they tell, a year came when he had only one man in his class, while the number of women had steadily increased. "Young gentleman," he would start off. Then, the story goes on, there was no man at all; "Q" dropped his salutation and talked as if he had no auditors in mind.

Not until after the end of the last war were women at Cambridge granted "Titles of Degrees," which means that to this day they are not granted degrees directly — only certificates to the effect that if they were men the work they have done would entitle them to a degree. Oxford, on the other hand, grants women degrees with all the rights and privileges that the superior sex at Cambridge reserves to itself. Everybody agrees that when this war is over Cambridge must succumb to the inevitable.

A University ordinance restricts the number of women in the colleges to five hundred — a tenth of the total peace-time registration. These five hundred are picked, through tough examinations, out of many times that number of applicants. The butterflies and the vamps haven't a chance to get in. One co-ed that I met soon after coming to Cambridge was "sent down" at the end of the first term; she had been too hospitable to men, both Greek and barbarian. A very hardworking and sensible co-ed in my class became engaged during the year to an engineer. They met while taking their turn at fire-watching at night. I asked her what percentage her state of bliss represents in her college. "About one per cent," she replied. "How do you figure that?" "Well, I am the only one." In peace times there are more love affairs, but Cambridge is nothing like the marriage market place that nearly any American university is. The young men are nothing like so distracted by co-eds; perhaps the campus belles, who are not co-eds, afford sufficient distraction. Young Britishers simply do not find young women so necessary as young Americans find them. Contrasting them with respect to women, one inclines to agree with that sophisticated Frenchman who declared Americans more preoccupied with sex than any other country on earth.

It seems to me that English boys are more beautiful than English girls, more beautiful also than American boys, whereas American girls are prettier than the English. Perhaps it is the sensitiveness of features that gives the impression. At a spritely college concert in which the young men played skits in addition to singing and making music, I looked at the finely chiseled, sensitive faces of the lads on the program and also in the audience and concluded that the portraits one sees of Shelley, Byron and other beautiful young English poets must be representative of the college breed. Their voices are toned down, but after you get to know them, you find their ideas are not. I am positive that if three instructors in Economics were fired in Cambridge, as they were in my own University not long ago, for having ideas on labor that did not comport with the ideas of a board of regents made up of oil millionaires and corporation lawyers, undergraduates would raise unmitigated hell. So would the country.

To an American the English educational system seems extraordinarily casual. The combination of casualness and formality in England is as remarkable as that between the dampness and coldness of its weather. The casualness somehow seems to have trained men to feel responsible towards society and "to serve God in church and state." Ph.D. worship in American universities and even in jerk-water colleges has destroyed casualness and substituted Ph.D. theses of Germanic methodicalness and pedestrian turgidity for books of brightness. The average Ph.D. thesis is nothing but a transference of bones from one graveyard to another. In English universities peadoggies and Education courses are still the tail to the dog, without benefit of laws to make all students training as teachers swallow its hair. The orthodox Professor of English Literature in America produces "studies" that only other professors can read. The professor of any literature in England writes essays that human beings in general can take pleasure in reading.

Books are all right in their place, but "a mighty bloodless substitute for life." A man simply is not a true Cambridge man if, when spring comes, he does not walk out on the Grantchester Meadows. Grantchester is just up the lazy Cam from Cambridge and there are two ways of getting there — by boat or along the public footpath. Grantchester is where you drink tea in gardens, or, if you choose, looking at odd murals adorning the glad verses that Rupert Brooke wrote about his native village —

> Stands the Church clock at ten to three?
> And is there honey still for tea? —

before he went to war and with his young body made "some corner of a foreign field forever England." The Green Man in Grantchester seldom runs out of whisky and never out of beer, they say. The Grantchester Meadows are early golden with buttercups, and then the grain fields beside them are red with poppies. From the sky overhead the larks pour down their liquid notes. When I have forgotten everything else about Cambridge, I'll still remember Grantchester and the Grantchester Meadows. There are other villages, and there are Madingley woods where the owls hoot and the green woodpeckers peck and the wild pigeons coo "I like my home, I do."

Sometimes during the long daylight after summer dinner, I like to go into the college garden and play bowls. You throw the white ball, the "jack," anywhere out on the grass and then try to hit it with the spheroid balls, biased so that you have to roll them in curves. There's something in the game freer and easier and more casual than playing bowls down an "alley." Bowling on the greensward while the sun is still shining at ten o'clock at night seems a part of Cambridge.

I like to hear the anecdotes that are always coming up about the odd characters that have maintained their oddities in Cambridge. They make me think of the characters that the ranch folks back home so love to tell about — Shanghai Pierce, W 6 Wright, old Seco Smith, Aunt Mary Givens and an Iliad of others. They had all their bark on and had never been smoothed down by art or learning, but somehow they and their rememberers always come to my memory when the Cambridge people begin talking about their characters.

There was the old Dean of Emmanuel who so loved his pipe that after he had entered the pulpit and got the congregation going on a hymn he would retire to his vestry for a few more comfortable puffs before taking up the burden of the sermon. Invariably, while the last verse was being sung, the vestryman would come and summon him. "Tell 'um to sing the last three verses over," the old Dean would say. "They likes their hymn and I likes my pipe." And he would puff on in comfort.

There was the professor they called "The Sick Buzzard." He must have looked like Ichabod Crane. P never was sick, but he had a habit of getting unsteady. One night while he was lurching up Trumpington Road he fell off into the miniature canal-way, with about two inches of water in it. Spluttering and splashing, he bawled out, "Save the women and children. I can swim." Another day he appeared with his head wrapped up. "What's the matter, P?" a solicitous soul asked. "Some bloody bloke trod on me ear last night," he growled.

There was the frenetical master of Trinity College, who, dying a long time ago, after many years of contention with the Fellows — the governing body of the college — willed that his body be buried in the antechapel so "that the Fellows may trample upon me dead, as they have done living." He was the opposite of Brit Bailey, who when he came to die on what is still called Bailey's Prairie in Brazoria County, Texas, willed that his coffin be buried standing upright, rifle by his side and a jug of whisky at his feet, "because I never have looked up to any man while living and when I'm gone I don't want anybody saying, 'Here *lies* old Brit Bailey.' "

There was terrific, tyrannical, withering, immensely learned Bentley, Master also of Trinity. At the end of a long executive session one of his fellow masters observed, "It is not yet quite clear to me," whereupon Bentley volunteered, "Are we then to wait until your mud has subsided?"

I'm mighty glad I came to Cambridge. I grew up among men who were always "going in pardners" and treating each other generously and decently — as decent pardners must treat each other if they are to get along and as decent pardners feel like treating each other anyhow. It is not only

their common language, their common inheritance of the
noblest literature on earth and many common material and
national interests that dictate a decent pardnership between
America and the British nations. It is a common civilization.
Whether I have added anything to common understanding,
I do not know. I do know I have been treated as generously,
as decently, as sincerely and as simply in the right, warming
way as ever the old-timey hospitable people back home,
so proud of their hospitality, have treated me. There's nothing else on earth so good as kind hearts and free minds.
Kind hearts and free minds are what Cambridge means
to me.

CHAPTER II
Glimpses of People

WHAT, after all the generations of play-writers, novelists, autobiographers, biographers, diarists, and other revealers, castigators and extollers of English character, can any man add? Nothing, except a few notes on how, at a time different from all other times, under circumstances peculiar to himself, an eyebrow has now and then lifted itself to him. Even the highest hope, as Lord Grey of Fallodon said concerning another subject, is that "those of us who have nothing new to tell may have something that is fresh to say."

I

The book entitled *English Folk,* woven by Wallace Notestein of Yale University out of biographical materials, opens with a modern odd-job laborer and runs back, character by character and generation by generation, to Elizabethan days. Notestein's idea is that certain pronounced common denominators of English life are to be found through the centuries and in all classes of people. He is right. Anybody who has read English literature from Chaucer on down meets in England now characters and characteristics recognizable from the past. This kind of thing is true in any country — and the known history of the human race is so brief that any philosopher might say, "Nothing human is foreign to me." Yet it would be easier to find in England today the men that Doctor Johnson bullied and loved than to find a George Washington in America.

English conduct in 1944 seems to me nearer to the modulated, controlled eighteenth century than to any other great age of the past. It seems nearer to that than to the on-top-of-the-world, bearing-the-white-man's-burden and also cap-lifting Victorian age. A rowdy, boisterous, swashbuckling Petruchio appearing anywhere in England these days would be as much out of his element as Ivanhoe. Sir Toby Belch, Falstaff, Mercutio, Drake and young gallants clanking their spurs down the aisles of Saint Paul's live on as English types by sheer vitality and expansiveness, but the "spacious times" of Queen Elizabeth have become an antiquity. "Nothing in excess," which the cultivated of the eighteenth century took from the Greeks as their code of conduct, has seeped downward to the nation. Not even singing is allowed in modern pubs, except in places like East London and among the lusty miners of South Wales. Whatever hangover from vaulting Elizabethan England struts about belongs to the extremes of society — to the Lord Louis Mountbatten privileged, really Commandos in civilian as well as military life, and to the unwashed and uncaring. The middle class has always been sober, and now its long process of pulling the Commandos down and the groundlings up into its respectabilities has about reached the climax.

In his sinewy chapter on "The Soul of England," Dean Inge queries if the divergent traits found in English life do not originate from the different classes, "the upper class being adventurous, active, ambitious and apt for governing others, while the lower class is unenterprising, slothful, noisy and emotional." It is possible that those Americans who feel constantly irritated because the lower classes do not make revolution do not know everything about what is good for either democracy or the English. Meantime the respectable middle class operates as inexorably as the mills of the gods.

If in the blacked-out night you hear rollicky voices singing anywhere in England, nine chances to ten they are American. A cultivated lady told me that two years ago she would have been shocked to hear such voices, now heard nightly on the streets of London, Manchester and other cities. I should add that many citizens have come to delight in them and to wish that more of them were native. This is not wishing for the impossible; a people may vary in temper from generation to generation without changing their essential nature. I think that Englishwomen incline more towards Elizabethan gusto than their men. They look sturdier on the whole, have sturdier manners. The old English families have been kept vigorous by careful selection of the females that the males breed to. Americans, conscious of the fact that they have the world by the tail with a downhill pull on it, and uninhibited by the cult for quiet manners, are more Elizabethan than the English.

This has nothing to do with bravery, stamina, tenacity.

The bulldog never howls one tenth so loud as the pot-
likker hound. The ideal of daring so often phrased by
Mr. Churchill has in this war been quietly acted out by a
hundred thousand Hotspur pluckers of bright honor leap-
ing into the ice of air and ocean, diving into volcanoes of
fire, performing little, nameless unremembered acts of duty
and decency.

The Lords in Parliament assembled sit on benches that
not even a legislator from Arkansas would look at — unless
he were electioneering among farmers. The Capitol at
Washington has more luxuries, paid for by the government, than any other statehouse in the world. One freezing morning I asked a charwoman at Cambridge if she
weren't cold, scrubbing with bare arms the floor of a room
colder than a cold storage plant. "Me arms get so cold,"
she said. "Then why don't you wear a coat?" I asked. "I
have to be free to work," she replied and went on scrubbing, and as I walked away I heard her singing. The boys
at Winchester School, noted for its recognition of brains
in individuals, sit on the same backless benches that pupils
used in the same rooms two hundred years ago. Many village houses are without running water even in the kitchen
— not unlike many farmhouses in our South. Comfort, with
the softening effect it is supposed to have on the human
system, is far less worshiped in England than among
Americans.

Wallace Notestein tells how the daughters of a wealthy
landlord, politician and improver of cattle breeds and of
land cultivation a hundred and fifty years ago "were
made strong by discipline. They were given simple food

and not allowed to have a fire in their bedrooms or a hearthrug in their schoolroom." The midwinter regime of one English school for girls calls for running naked through a stone hall and jumping into a pool of cold water. The water can't be so cold as the hall however. The Arctic explorer Nansen was once asked if he had not suffered from cold in the far North. "No," he replied, "before I went north I had become accustomed to English bedrooms." The Cavendishes, according to Notestein, "invariably hunted, whatever the weather; the Duke seemed to think it a test of manhood to go shooting regardless of the elements." Thomas Bewick, great English wood engraver, born near the Scottish border in 1753, delighted as a youth in the society of farm laborers. From one of them, a man with stern-looking brows, high cheekbones, quick eyes, and longish visage, Thomas learned what he knew of astronomy. "I think I see him yet," he remembered, "sitting on a mound or seat by the hedge of his garden, regardless of the cold, and intent upon viewing the heavenly bodies." What may not the viewers of chaste celestial bodies, as cold as abstract virtue itself, miss by viewing them from the steam-heated comforts of Lick Observatories?

Mark Twain complained of a lack of anecdotes among passengers on an ocean voyage. Americans were absent, was his explanation. The modern anecdote among Hollywood-adoring, radio-stupefied Americans is apt to smell of Hedda Hopper gossip, Walter Winchell pre-war smartness, radio jokesmiths, and beer-bottle horseplay. Old-time pioneer stock, people I have cultivated all my life, are the best tellers of character anecdotes that I know. And character anecdotes are the best anecdotes in the world. The English and the Scotch and the Irish always have been meaty with anecdotes. They still are.

An old woman in a village in Cambridgeshire was drawing the warrant for her first old-age pension.

"Your ticket to heaven," the clerk said, handing it to her with a patronizing smile.

"Not exactly a ticket," the old woman replied, taking the warrant, "but it will make the waiting room a little more comfortable."

An old London woman was in bed in an upstairs room that was sheared half off by a bomb one night. Rescuers found her still in bed and insisted on taking her to better quarters. She refused to budge until her stockings had been found and brought to her so that she could put them on before stepping out.

While German guns were firing their final shots across the Channel to the Dover coast, a reporter found an old woman polishing her brass as she had polished it daily for fifty years, although not a window in her house was left with a shard of glass.

"No need to have dirty brass," she remarked, "even if we don't have any windows."

Connie dispenses fluids ranging from tea to whisky, each in its hour, at a club bar in London. She was telling me how she sleeps through the pilotless bomb assaults. "I figure," she said, "that I am just one in seven millions of people and there's no use staying awake to see if I'm elected. If I don't sleep I can't work, and I've got to work." The worst time she ever had was during the big blitz. "The Jerries were coming over thick and fast and dropping plenty. My mother was getting highly nervous about them. Grannie was staying with us and she was all upset. One really bad night I had just about all I could do. I was playing cards with my six-year-old child and making him think the explosions were great fun. I was keeping Grannie pacified on tea — I really don't know how she managed to swallow so much, but she kept on swallowing and was all right as long as she didn't stop. And I had to keep my mother talking. It would have been fatal to let her stop, listen and think. The next day my stomach turned wrong side out."

In the eighteenth century two brothers of the Cavendish family, "famous for dignity and reticence," stopped one night at an inn and were ushered into a bedroom with three four-poster beds. One of the beds had the curtains drawn around it. Before getting into his own bed, the older brother went over to the drawn curtain, held his candle up, and looked inside. He redrew the curtains and said nothing. Presently the other brother walked over also, drew the curtains, looked in, closed the curtains, and said nothing. Then they blew out their candles and went to sleep. The next day on the road each remarked to the other that he had seen a corpse in the curtained bed. This is English reticence.

It makes me think of a story of a noted old stagedriver

named John Dunn at Taos, New Mexico. Before there was
any road to speak of, he used to drive passengers up to
Taos over the mountains from the railroad many hours'
journey away. One morning he took on a load of four or
five passengers, among them a woman of pathfinder inclinations who insisted on sitting with him on the driver's
seat. She began by exclaiming at the scenery, soon pro-
gressed to cautioning him at steep places and, in between,
machine-gunned a barrage of questions that showed more
ignorance than sensible curiosity. At the end of the journey
the passengers got out and a quiet man asked what the
fare was. "Two and a half," the old rawhide replied. Each
passenger paid, the pathfinder woman coming last. She
handed over a five-dollar bill. John Dunn put it in his
pocket and turned away.

"Where's my change?" she asked.

"Ain't any."

"But you told the others the fare was two and a half."

"They didn't talk."

The English have done plenty of talking about their
way of proceeding according to habit — not "according to
plan." They take a kind of pride in the planless, casual, ac-
cidental way in which the British Empire grew up, and it
most emphatically did grow up in a way opposite to the
deadly methodicalness with which Hitler's Germans
planned for the German Empire to dominate the world
(including all the Americans). People sometimes mistake
English casualness for stiffness, or even for cold indifference. Casualness can be terribly disconcerting, espe-

cially if you are so heated up that you want everybody else to be.

The nearest approach to volubility that some Englishmen make is in expressing their own reticence. One evening Scottish J. M. Barrie, whom Peter Pan is not likely to let die, and A. E. Housman, who taught Latin at Cambridge while he restrained the Shropshire Lad, sat together at dinner and then at wine without saying anything. The next day Barrie wrote a note: —

Dear Professor Housman: I am very sorry about last night, when I sat next to you and did not say a word. You must have thought I was a very rude man; I am really a very shy man. Sincerely yours, J. M. BARRIE.

Reply came back at once: —

Dear Sir James Barrie: I am sorry about last night, when I sat next to you and did not say a word. You must have thought I was a very rude man; I am really a very shy man. Sincerely yours, A. E. HOUSMAN.

The day after the invasion opened, June 6, I met an English friend who still suffers from wounds received as an infantryman in the last war. I said, "I feel in a kind of daze. The facts are too stupendous to be comprehended." He replied, "I suppose there are a certain number of people who have suspended work until things settle down a bit." He was not suspending his work. Yet I know him to be made out of nerves. He will explode on some such subject as the lackeydom of climbers who are fortifying themselves in snug home nests while their betters disappear into obscurity — or eternity — in remote parts of the earth, fighting the war. If the earth were cracking under his feet, he might suspend his round of daily duties in order to help build a bridge across the crack so as to carry on the duties over the chasm.

On the evening of the same day I went down on the Cam River to hear the Cambridge Madrigal Singers give their annual concert. They were in boats, and their voices coming down the water and over the gardened lawns and up into the trees were beautiful. I say up into the trees, for the cawing rooks up there seemed to enjoy it. From my point of view, a bawling bull calf in a paddock against the river added to the harmony; so did two little colts frisking about their grazing mothers, and a thrush that turned himself completely loose. Every few minutes zebra-striped Mustangs, Lightnings and Thunderbolts, painted for the invasion, would whizz by overhead, and in a way they also added to the harmony. The singers did not seem to notice them any more than nightingales notice barrage guns.

The mother of a young English scientist working in a Washington laboratory said to me, "Our son writes that most of the men he is working with over there are forty years old and older." Then she added, "Nearly all our scientists are very young or very old. In the last war most of the young men going in for science were killed." They volunteered, in fact, for the most dangerous jobs, jobs often that they were not the best fitted to do. They were not selected, sorted out, for technical work as young scientists have been directed in this war by the British and American governments, and by Germany as well.

I know who started the lie that every Englishman will stand till the last Frenchman dies. I could say who has been most agile in repeating it in America. The most moving war memorial — and every village and town in Britain has its memorial of the last war — I have seen anywhere is in Trinity College Chapel, Cambridge. As you enter the anteroom, you see the figures of Newton, Bacon, Macaulay, Tennyson — not that Trinity is lacking in other notabilities. Walking down the long, dimly lit chapel, you come to an inscription on the marble tiles of the altar floor. It reads: IN MEMORY OF THE MEN OF THIS COLLEGE WHO GAVE THEIR LIVES IN WAR, MCMXIV–MCMXVIII. Then on twenty-six panels, thirteen to each side, you see the names engraved. Six hundred and fifty of them, in alphabetical order, good names plain and strong, plainly engraved. Six hundred and fifty from only one, though it is the largest, of the score or so of colleges that make up Cambridge University. I cannot convey the feeling of national tragedy expressed by those lists reaching up to the stained windows along the lofty walls and back into the shadows of the altar. These young men and others like them from colleges all over the land were to have been the leaders. Well —

> If blood be the price of admiralty,
> Lord God, we ha' paid in full!

2

One May morning that promised the whole earth and the fullness thereof, my friend Captain Winford Burke and I set out for the races at Newmarket. This is not a story about horses, and I had as well say in the beginning that they were very beautiful running on the straightaway, green-turfed track against meadows as green as new mesquite leaves. It struck me how in America circular tracks are for the advantage of spectators at the expense of the horses, and how in England the straight tracks are for the advantage of horses at the expense of the spectators. As always, there were plenty of hot tips, the hottest ones coming from a pair of American sergeants whose camp gave them daily access to the stables. But Burke and I were looking for far, far better things.

On the platform at Cambridge, where we went to take the train, there were crowds of people; there always are. As I started into an open car door, a bareheaded man dressed in a blue suit blocked it. He appeared to be undecided as to whether to go on inside or to get out; he just stood blocking the door. Other people pressed up, not, as I later recalled, crowding him so much as crowding me. In a minute or two nobody, not even I, was trying to get into the door. As I turned to Burke, I felt for my wallet in my inside coat pocket. It wasn't there. The bustling little crowd had disappeared like a covey of chick partridges. The wallet, a horse's head tooled on it, a gift from

El Paso, contained a card bearing my name and Cambridge address, also five pounds in notes — twenty dollars.

The train still had a few minutes to leave. We reported to a policeman — at the remotest standing space on the platform. He said that the pickpockets work as a gang and that they would throw the wallet away. We went through the train but could not find the bareheaded man in blue and the accomplice I recollected at my right elbow. A dozen people had warned me that all the scum and toughs of London come to the races to prey on the innocent. They say that "virtue is its own reward," but a man hates to be even occasionally reminded of what a fool he constantly is. Three days later there was a knock at my door. A middle-aged woman and her daughter came in. The elder one handed me the wallet. Her husband, a railroad employee, had found it, empty of everything but the identification card, under a railroad bridge on the edge of Cambridge, in the direction of Newmarket. I was certainly glad to get the wallet back, but the voluntary act of honor and honesty gave me more pleasure than the loss of the money gave me displeasure.

Often as I walk by allotment vegetable plots on public land accessible to everybody, I am struck by how nobody steals a ripe tomato or an exposed onion. The Arts Theatre in Cambridge has a roof garden to which people between acts repair with beer mugs and cheerful chatter. During wartime summers, this roof garden grows plants burdened with reddening tomatoes. Now, what is better with beer than a tangy tomato? And who is less inclined to quibble over ownership than a bevy of theatergoers? But nobody appropriates a single one of those unwatched tomatoes. I see nothing but popular honesty to prevent wholesale cheating on the London tubes. The charge for a ride is according to distance. One buys a ticket for whatever price he chooses, rides as far as he wants to, surrenders the ticket to a collector at his destination. Often neither light nor time gives the collector opportunity to inspect the ticket. I have not seen a single ticket holder called down for having cheated. The presumption is that few of the millions of riders in the tubes cheat on their fares. Where the great majority are honest, the average person with dishonest inclinations is kind of badgered and shamed into conformity. At a counter where several grades of some article, soap for instance, are for sale, the clerk, unless the purchaser specifies, makes a practice of offering the lowest priced variety. The clerks have evidently made no study of how to influence people. Yet a tin-horn treatise on the practice of tin-horn "influence" sells also in England.

I always did believe in economizing on haircuts and hotel breakfasts. The Christmas holidays had come before I paid my second visit to a hairdresser. The first haircut was in Cambridge and cost twenty cents; the second was in London and cost fifty cents, with a tip. The essential difference between the two was sanitation and conversation. The Cambridge hairdresser's shop is upstairs and I did not know what it was like until I got inside. The hairdresser's name is advertised as Jolly, but he should have been baptized as Master Silence. He is deft with scissors and clippers. I approve of being silent when a body has nothing to say. Also I approve of the shilling price. My head and I both came out of the operation just as well off as if we had been in a big barber shop paneled with mirrors, floored with tile, fitted up with head-steamers, electric massage machines, a blaring radio and supernumerary flunkies to yank at a patron's coattail. The fact that Master Silence knows his business and has no radios and other paraphernalia to run up the cost to his customers makes me willing to grow another crop of hair for his deliverance.

The London shop opens onto the street and seems to invite entrance. The hairdresser into whose booth I ventured, curtained off from other booths to give privacy, had an eager look. As soon as he had me in his chair he began to demonstrate both his desire and his ability to talk. He opened up with commentaries on the extraordinarily realistic speech lately made by General Smuts. From that he went to Lord Kitchener of the last war, whose hair he used to trim. "You're busy," he reported himself as saying to some of Kitchener's staff while he waited for the General to place his head under the scissors. "Oh, no," the staff would reply, "we have nothing to do. General Kitchener does it all." The barber said that Kitchener finally got so high up in his tower that nobody could tell him anything. He was contrasting Kitchener with Eisenhower and Montgomery. He has not cut their hair, but he knows a lot about them. Like everybody else in this country that I have talked to, he is mighty well satisfied with the choice of Eisenhower as commander-in-chief of the Allied armies.

Mullet is the barber's name. He talked about the decay of France, which General Smuts stressed. He talked about

German sea power. He glanced at the subject of central heating, awaiting devolopments in Britain. His information was seasoned with a pinch or two of wit, especially when he described how a soldier in his outfit in the last war set a can on a hot stove upstairs in France, how the can turned out to contain petrol instead of water, how an officer cut off from the stairs by the fire broke his neck sliding down the roof, and how a private saved his neck by merely sticking his head out the window to breathe fresh air until a ladder was brought. Mr. Mullet talked like a man and not a puppet. He reflected the reading that seasons experience. I resolved to save some of my hair for another visit to him. His shop has no radio either. His talk is worth the extra bob and sixpence. I like talk when a man has something to say even better than I like no talk when he has nothing to say.

While this barber cut my hair on another occasion, he told me about a bishop he had had in thrall. "This bishop wore knee breeches and did not look as if he had suffered from food rationing. I said to him, 'Now that I have you seated where you can't get away, I'm going to give you some of your own medicine. I am going to preach you a sermon. The subject of it is Hate. You preachers are always talking about loving your neighbors. How can you be practical in loving your neighbor without hating his enemy? We ought to hate the hateful and be intolerant of the intolerable. A man with strong feelings for the good is going to have strong feelings against evil. You preachers that are afraid of hate are afraid of anything strong.'" I knew that the Germans were coming into the sermon and they did.

The day was cloudy and while I sat listening to Mullet and his scissors, the Alert went on and we could hear a pilotless bomb droning somewhere. I asked Mullet if he was sleeping in a shelter these days. "No, sir," he replied, "when this war started, I said that Hitler was not going to order me where to sleep, and I have slept in my own bed consistently."

He went on to tell me about a woman he saw hurrying to a bus stop. She was followed by a girl maybe ten years old carrying several bundles. They were so heavy that they kept the girl from hurrying, and the bus left before she reached it. The woman, much put out, began abusing the child. "I couldn't stand it," Mullet said. "I told her that she should be horsewhipped for two reasons — first, for not carrying the bundles herself and, second, for abusing the child. I don't know whether this was her own child or not. I hope not, for I wouldn't want her breed to increase."

Mullet is his brother's keeper; yet he has no desire to regulate people. It is a marvel to me how he burns and burns without being consumed. In a lifetime I have not met a more independent democrat — or a better barber.

Proud with reason the English are of Montgomery and their fighting armies. Proud, with reverence and gratitude, of the R.A.F. But when the Navy sinks the *Scharnhorst* or performs some other good deed, any stranger in the land can tell where English hearts lie. These people have been going down to ships upon the sea and out to sea and over the sea for so many, many generations since their ancestors "espoused the everlasting sea" that their hearts are seagoing too. With them, as Conrad wrote, "man and sea interpenetrate." On the wall of that "fairest, good-liest and most famous parish church," Saint Mary Red-cliffe, in Bristol, these words of antique nobility report of Admiral Penn, father to Quaker William: "AND THUS HE TOOK LEAVE OF THE SEA HIS OLD ELEMENT." Joe Mercer, sixty-four, coxswain of a lifeboat that has saved hundreds of lives in the English Channel during the war years, ad-mitted that he would be glad when the German guns twenty miles away ceased firing. Why hadn't he left this "Hell Corner"? "It's the sea," he answered simply. "I could no more spend two or three days away from the sea than I could fly."

When Captain Frederick John Walker, ace U-boat killer of the Royal Navy and commander of the Second Escort Group made up of the *Starling, Woodpecker, Kite, Magpie* and *Wild Goose,* approached Liverpool early this year with his sloops, the Royal Marines played them into the harbor, flags flew and the First Lord of the Admiralty was there to greet them. So was the Captain's wife. All over the land hearts sent up a cheer that echoed the days of Drake and Nelson. A submarine on which the eldest Walker son served was one that did not come back. Captain Walker had been decorated for his technical skill as well as for superb huntsmanship of German wolfpacks. His men said he could smell a U-boat for miles; then it was hoist the signal "General chase," with which Lord Howard at-tacked the Armada; fire on the submarine; ram it, depth-charge it, hound it. Not long after his greatest victory, he died ashore in bed, on a Sunday, from a heart attack trace-able to unflaggingly arduous services. He was only forty-seven. They held services for him in a cathedral and then they took his body to sea, where all good seamen go. Had he lived to retire, he would no doubt have raised prize roses, perhaps debated between dahlias and lavender in a certain place, probably experimented with a cross between greengages and Victoria plums. And night and day, often when he did not know it, when perhaps he was smiling at the goldfinches swinging the sunflower heads in his garden, John Masefield's "Sea Fever" would have been throbbing in his heart.

3

On the afternoon of the longest day of the year, I sit by a coal fire smoking a pipe and not grumbling at the weather. There are heavy clouds and the wind is out of the north as it has been most of the days for two weeks, making our invasion operations more difficult and making the achievements of the operators more admirable. I have just had a visit from a fine old English gentleman, a doctor of medicine past eighty. After he had got his legs comfortably positioned and filled his pipe, he recalled how Emerson and Carlyle sat all one evening before a fire saying nothing and how when at last Emerson rose to go he broke the silence by remarking, "This has been one of the most genial evenings within my memory."

I told the doctor that when I build my fireplace I am going to have a sentence out of Frederic Remington's *Sundown Leflare* graved on the mantel. Sundown and another mountain man cooked and ate their supper. "Then," says Remington, "they sat down with the greatest philosopher on earth — the fire."

My spritely old friend and I sat by the fire and talked. He said, as I have heard scores, perhaps hundreds, of other people in this country say with deep conviction, that mutual understanding between America and the British nations is to be desired almost as much as victory over the enemy. He quoted the great philosopher Spinoza: "I make it my business not to make people angry, not to laugh at them, but to seek to understand them."

I sit here by the fire in a comfort that seems immoral and shameful when I think of our men — and by "our men" I mean the British as well as American — dying and fighting on day and night, without sleep or ready food. The pilotless bombs destroying London homes do nothing to the spirits of the people but strengthen them. I have come to the conclusion that an Englishman will hardly shed tears over a personal sorrow, will not feel sorry for himself, but when it comes to the land he has been planted in for so many centuries and loves for its spiritual as well as material qualities, it is quite different.

"If anything should happen to me," a soldier twenty-one years old wrote back to his sweetheart from Burma — just before he was killed — "remember that I always loved things that were right and true and faithful. . . . Forget about me mostly, but think of me sometimes as one who loved England and the better parts of man."

Rupert Brooke was representing millions when he wrote the threnody of the last war: —

If I should die, think only this of me:
That there's some corner of a foreign field
That is for ever England. There shall be
In that rich earth a richer dust concealed;
A dust whom England bore, shaped, made aware,
Gave, once, her flowers to love, her ways to roam,
A body of England's breathing English air,
Washed by the rivers, blest by suns of home.

I want to quote a newspaper poem entitled "Forts Going Out," by an R.A.F. man from Gloucestershire named John Moore.

To-day I watched the Forts go out to their great hazards,
Rising in terrible flocks from the green English meadows,
In wide circles mounting like huge birds, like buzzards,
While the hedgerow finches fled from their flying shadows.

They filled the still air with throbbing and thunderous clamour
As I stood and watched by the gate into Jacob's Lane,
And I thought, There go Texas, Oregon, Oklahoma,
Michigan, Massachusetts, Vermont, Florida, Maine.

High-hearted out of England's heart towards their grim missions
In perilous skies rising from the green English land, —
And I watched them till their great flock became in the distance
A small cloud the size of a man's hand.

I watched, and my heart lifted, while the sky throbbed and thundered,
And slowly the quiet crept back to field and farm,

And the Forts were as small as a gaggle of geese, as the white-
    fronted
Heralds of wild winds, harbingers of storm.

And now I wait as one waits for a homecomer,
Till they, who are close to our hearts, come back again
To the heart of England, Texas, and Oklahoma,
Idaho, Oregon, Michigan, Vermont, Maine.

The clouds have broken now, and I hear the roar of
destiny as Forts fly Hitleriteward. Citizens feel so intensely
towards the airmen and talk about them so much partly
because they alone of the fighting men are visible. And
during long years they have been going, going, many of
them never coming back, while the infantry, the artillery,
the tanks and other ground forces gathered strength and
trained. An American major attached to a British army
corps says that last winter they had no fires in their tin
huts. There wasn't enough coal for all the British and all
the American forces, and at least some of the British went
without.

Doctor Pritchard looks fiftyish. I met him in the dark
days of last November. I had rushed out of a lighted room
about eight o'clock one night. Without pausing to accus-
tom my eyes to the blackout, I rammed myself into a
cornice that knocked the breath out of me. About three
days later I decided that I had either broken a rib or mashed
one of my lungs. Slight of body, bright of eye and face,
and gay, but quiet of voice, Doctor Pritchard brought into
my room more sunshine than any English winter could
afford. He said a rib was only bruised and taped me up. I

felt new-made and wore that tape until I came near having to call him to do some skin grafting. Then three or four weeks later I took to moping with what was probably influenza — result of that science-defying amalgamation of dampness, chilliness and stone walls of antiquity. Doctor Pritchard came again and brought sunshine. He paid several calls, though he and all other doctors were rushed to exhaustion in those days.

Along after New Year's I asked my Cambridge mentor if the doctor would not send a bill. "He'll send it eventually," the mentor said. I had learned that bills are often as slow in arriving over here as they are from that old Southern gentleman-styled hotel, the Driskill in Austin. May its shadow and that of its courtly host never grow less! . . . After waiting three months, I decided to call on Doctor Pritchard. I just wanted to see him anyhow. In front of a fire in a room with two bright pictures and a graceful ship model in it, he began telling me about two Texans, oilmen, he knew in Persia. One of them was very quiet, never said anything, and had the reputation of being a dangerous man; the other talked a lot and talked loud and one day missed twelve six-shooter shots at a beer bottle.

It took me several minutes to get to my bill. "I never keep books," Doctor Pritchard laughed. Then he began telling me about the prisoner of war who made the beautiful sailing sloop. . . . I got back to the bill again.

"Oh," he said, "I wouldn't think of charging an American. You all are over here, you know. There is too much charging going on. We hear about it, and it's a bloody shame." (As a matter of fact, there is less overcharging of American soldiers in England than there is in American cities frequented by them.) "I never have charged an American and I won't."

"I'll have to get even with you somehow," I said.

"No, it is not a matter of getting even with me. The account has been balanced."

I raised my hand at the throb of a great formation of Fortresses coming home from the Continent.

His keen face brightened. "Oh, what a sight a great flight of them makes going out in the morning," he said. "I always salute them."

"Yes, I do too," I said. "The roar can never be routine. It is the same at night when the R.A.F. goes out."

"When I hear them at night, I go out in the garden and wave to them and wish them good luck. They can't see me. They don't know I am there, but my heart is with them just the same."

This made me tell him how for years now I have never seen a bright moon, or the moon at all, without thinking of the R.A.F. and giving them a salute in my soul. Often nowadays they don't want a moon and with their path-finders they find the target in clouded darkness. But the R.A.F. moon will, as long as I live, be as real to me as the "Comanche moon" was to the frontiersmen of the South-west.

I went to a bookstore and, with instructions for proper delivery, bought a copy of a certain book. On the fly-leaf of it I wrote: *"Brightness falls from the air — where Doctor S. H. Pritchard walks. This is a salute to his gal-*

lantry and generosity from an American whose life he has brightened."

But that American does not imagine that twelve shillings and sixpence worth of book has evened up the doctor's bill.

4

In the people must be anybody's trust. English people, carrying unwrapped loaves of bread and market baskets in the street, gathering dandelions into a pan alongside a lane, thatching a stack of wheat, lugging sacks of coal into a cellar or quarters of beef into a butcher shop, standing in patient, weary, cheerful line for a bus at the close of day, holding babies and buying savings stamps at the always crowded post office window, going about in queer clothes without the least self-consciousness — somehow they often remind me of the independent Indians, never apologizing for their existence, standing wrapped in their blankets before fashion windows on the finest avenue in Mexico City.

Little things, little people. The wife and six-year-old son of one of the college porters sniffled quietly in the porter's lodge over the killing of their dog by an automobile. He comforted them most patiently. Another porter, who used to smell of whisky stronger than horseradish until whisky for civilians became scarcer than hen's teeth, thanked me for a cigar, which a soldier had given me.

"Oi'll keep this tul Sunday," he said in his slow, thick voice, "and smoke it after lunch sitting in me daughter's parlor." He told me how a cigar manufacturer once gave him a cigar wrapped in tinfoil and explained that it was especially wrapped to sell for fifty cents to members of Parliament, but, not wrapped, was just a common cigar. He asked me if I had read the University Sermon for last Sunday, printed in the *Cambridge Review*. I hadn't and he exhorted me to read it. "There's something in it about the black men."

Little things. On a peaceful Sunday morning while I was walking to buy newspapers I saw a private soldier in R.A.F. blue and a girl in WAAF blue looking upward at a cat on a high wall and talking to it. It came down to be stroked and then, when they moved on, it followed the length of its home premises. A man in a narrow side street was delivering bottles of milk from a cart drawn by a chunky bay pony with longish mane — probably the wild-roaming, hardy Dartmoor breed. The milkman walked from door to door, the pony following. While he went inside, I petted the animal's gentle head. "A mighty nice pony you have," I said as he came up. . . . "Ah," and his eyes lighted, "isn't she a charming thing!" . . . "I wish I had an apple for her," I said. . . . "She would thank you."

Along my way to tea in a cottage, a mallard duck with five little ones gave life to a drainage canal. Two girls pitched in bits of bread. The mother duck would come only halfway across the canal towards them and then would turn

back. She picked up only the crumbs fallen on her side.
After the girls had cast in all they had, and moved on, the
duck retrieved what remained afloat. Her stalwartness was
comical, also English. At the cottage I met a white hen
that spends a large part of her life on the back porch waiting and hoping for a door to be left open so that she can
walk into the parlor.

Berryripe time, and I passed a clump of elderberries,
small trees, in which starlings were gorging themselves and
making a cheerful music hardly classifiable as song. While
I watched them, a stalwart woman came up with a basket
on her arm and paused to look also.

"The starlings are certainly enjoying the berries," I said.

"Elderberries are good against flies," she said.

"How?"

"Just carry a branch into the house and flies won't come
near them. I took home a sprig from one of these trees
the other day but it wasn't big enough. On the way back
I'm going in through that open gate and get a larger
branch. The owner doesn't mind."

The elders grow in a diminutive patch of ground next
to a store building. There are few window screens in England. The fly season is very brief. We walked on down the
narrow street towards the market square.

"Elderberries are good to make an ointment out of," the
woman said. "You take some lard and mix the berries with
it and boil. The ointment is fine for sores, chilblains, anything. There just isn't any better ointment. But, of course,
we can't spare the lard these days."

"Did you ever try mixing raw eggs and turpentine?" I asked.

"No. And did you ever drink any elderberry wine? Of course, we can't get the sugar now to make it. It is delicious, mostly homemade. Well, the birds won't go short this year."

We were at the corner.

"Good-by."

"Good-by."

She went her cheerful way, and mine was more cheerful for the encounter.

I got on a bus about dark in London to catch the train at Liverpool Street. At any time of day the Liverpool Station is the grimiest and most darksome in the world; in the blackout it is the heart of darkness. There are devious ways of getting into it from the streets, and it is as easy to enter it on the wrong side as on the right side. I knew that the bus would stop on the wrong side, and was particular in asking the conductress to let me know when to get off.

"I will show you," a woman on the opposite seat said. "We are getting off there also."

She got off with four children, her mother and another woman that might have been her grandmother. They were plainly "laboring people." She wanted to know what train I was taking, so that she could direct me to the proper side of the platform. The oldest of the children, a bright girl of about twelve, wanted to carry my suitcase, though of course I wouldn't let her. To the very young the grey-

haired always seem tottering on the edge of the grave. The
cortège escorted me through the dungeon-like entrance to
where there was a little light. Then the guiding spirit
pointed out about sixty steps away a railed stair that I
was to ascend for the bridge that would lead me across to
my platform. That was not enough, however. She made a
gesture to the girl, and the skipping one led me to the
very stairs. As I started up I waved her good-by; I paused
to see her join the family group; then with a wave all of
them disappeared into the dungeon-like entrance. They
were not taking any train. Probably they lived in this part
of the city. Their natural goodness of heart led them to
go out of their way to help a stranger.

One more picture — and *honi soit qui mal y pense*.
Late one night after the college gate was closed, an American soldier brought Mary Lee to my room, just to visit.
She is a telephone operator; two days before they had met
by chance over the telephone and made a blind date. I
noted at once her quiet refinement and lovely voice. She
talked easily, showing a clear mind, a cultivated taste and
a settled, serene kind of rebellion against the capitalistic
government of the land she loves. She is nineteen years
old and was transferred by the Ministry of Labour from
her home in Newcastle to Cambridge. Her father is forty-
four years old and was without work for fourteen years.
During that time he had forty cents a week dole money
for each of three children. By Wednesday night of each
week, winter as well as summer, there was no coal and no
fire; by Friday, no food. The five lived in two rooms.

There were no books in the home, but she went to school for ten years.

From children who did have books and the graces of life in their homes, from teachers, from the public library and from something innate, she developed a taste for beautiful and gentle things, particularly poetry and music. She had five years of French and does not like the French genius; she received a good grounding in Latin and German. She won a scholarship and would like to learn more. She has no hope of a college education. To save bus fare, she walks three miles from lodging to work four times a day, spending two thirds of her hour and a half at noon going to and from lunch. She is allowing one of her beautiful teeth to decay while she saves money for a holiday in London. At Newcastle she converted other telephone girls to the idea of socializing property. She thinks the masses of the British poor — and in proportion to the population they are very numerous and very poor — may be too weary after the war is at long last over to rise and claim their rights. She is not an agitator. I wish I could convey the evenness, the tolerance and the sad brightness of her talk.

I did not learn all I am telling from one visit. The clock was striking the hour when I saw her and the soldier out the locked doors. As they went away in the darkness they seemed to me as lost in this harsh world as two feathers in a remorseless wind from the bitter north. At dark a week later, just as I was going to dinner, a porter stopped me with word that a lady had called. It was Mary Lee to tell me good-by, she said, for she had learned that I was leaving very soon. I suggested dinner at a hotel. It was over the coffee that she told me about Fred, the fighter pilot to whom she was engaged and who was going to take her back to America. He cared more for his plane than for himself. He was German born, having been brought by his parents to Missouri when a year old. He was over six feet tall, blond, with "a cruel mouth." He delighted in fighting the Germans, and the Germans killed him. "He did not think he would ever be killed. I had no idea I was telling him good-by forever when he went out the last time."

After dinner we went to see the film of Noel Coward's *This Happy Breed* — the latter, ironic, part of it. From the cinema, without mentioning time or place, we walked back to my rooms. She told me about a wife-beater who put up a memorial window to his wife, not killed with kindness, in a church. She said that at seventeen she first learned about men from a businessman who had a wife and two children and who invited her to his office on a Sunday to get some eggs. He was the first man to tell her she was "not human." I asked her how human she is towards the soldiers she has consorted with, not trying to forget, since Fred's death. "Not too human," she said. Talk led to a poem by Rupert Brooke. On the table lay an anthology I had kept, from the books boxed for shipping, to carry in my suitcase. She had read only the first lines of "The Soldier"; the others she now read half aloud. "Can one still buy this book?" she asked. "It belongs to you," I said. Somehow it did. At midnight I told her that I would walk with her to the river on her long way home.

I did not feel as father to her, as brother, as belated gallant, as philosopher in mantle of kindness, or as the reporter

I have turned myself into. On the deserted street in the mist I remembered within myself Maurya in Synge's *Riders to the Sea* keening over the drowned ones beside the ever-lastingly relentless surf: "May the Almighty God have mercy on Bartley's soul, and on Michael's soul, and on the souls of Sheamus and Patch, and Stephen and Shawn; and may He have mercy on my soul, Nora, and on the soul of everyone left living in the world."

When we stopped on the bridge, it seemed to me that she was as "all alone without any company" as the latest lier-down to sleep in the cold ground. I told her good-by, and she told me good-by with lips that belong to Fred.

Ships that pass in the night. And you who are comfortable, relent a little towards the millions of girls over all the lands between all the seas of the world to whom these dragging years of wars, while taking from, have also given something of the realities. In taking away the dew from their eyes, experiences have made some callous, some foolish, some wise, too wise, many gay for a night, many sad for long, and all mysterious with the mysteries — and with the pities — of the human soul.

CHAPTER III
Two Lords and a Dog

I CAN'T PROVE IT, but it is my belief that within the present century Americans have come to chatter more than they formerly did. There were plenty of chatterers back in the days when Mark Twain rode on a stagecoach with a woman who described herself as "a pretty sociable heifer." Pioneer life always made some individuals, starved for talk, unlock their word-hoards when they got an occasional chance. Still, they were probably more hungry for talk from the outside world than to talk themselves. My mother tells about a man, a neighbor of her family in South Texas seventy years ago, who would take his gun, ride horseback out to a seldom-traveled road and hold up freighters in order to make them come to his ranch and partake of his hospitality so that he could "get the news."

The overwhelming increase of modern mechanical noises seems to have increased the proportion of Americans who regard silence as leaden rather than golden, and who take it for granted that no banality or triviality they can voice will be regarded otherwise than as a boon by any possible listener. Their chitter is involuntary, like that of prairie dogs, without connection between mouth and brain. A lot of them would be afraid of going down into the Grand Canyon without the moronic patter of a radio to accompany them, and then with the radio would never enter into the grandeur of the Canyon at all. Many blessings are disguised. Americans of this kind are probably responsible in part for the national idea — pure folklore — that Doctor Johnson's fellow countrymen do not talk. The great number of Americans in England during recent years has made the English self-conscious about their own reticence on trains and has brought out a great deal of English commentary on the subject. You meet the commentary constantly in newspapers as well as among citizens.

Cambridge is something over fifty miles from London. There are numerous trains a day, generally crowded, G. I.'s making up a strong per cent of the passengers. When I go "up to London," I really go "down," so far as direction is concerned, but no matter from what direction you approach London, you "go up." In France during the last war I learned to like the compartment arrangement of passenger coaches. An aisle runs the length of the car on one side against windows; each of the several compartments opens, with a sliding glass door, into it. Some of the English coaches provide an outside door to each compartment so that passengers can get on and off without having to file through the aisle. Some of the third-class coaches have no aisles but are partitioned into non-communicating compartments, an outside door at each end, or side. Railroad coaches in England are not so standardized as in America. The typical first-class compartment is designed to seat six passengers, three on one side and three on the other, facing each other. Four can sit comfortably on each row, however. I have been one of six in a row; nobody as broad as Gilbert K. Chesterton was present.

Lord Porter is a Fellow of Emmanuel College and has kept his book-stocked rooms there since he was bombed out of London. One morning early we started for London together. When we stepped into a compartment on the train, we found Lord Macmillan already seated and reading *The Times*. I had met him two days before while he acted as master of ceremonies in presenting, as a gift from the Pilgrim Society, Sir Isaac Newton's personal library — preserved fairly intact all these centuries — to Trinity College. Both these Lords are justices of the highest court of the British Empire and have been elevated to the peerage for outstanding competence and accomplishments in the legal profession.

The seats were all filled immediately. Presently I glanced up from my newspaper to see Porter, who was sitting next to the aisle, on his feet inviting a woman in the aisle to come inside. We made room for her on our seat. She produced a cigarette but lacked a light. I had one of the rare matches. Shortly a young lady appeared with a little dog, and room was made for her on the opposite seat. A heavy-set, well-preserved, dark man stood at the door in the aisle. There were other standers-up in the passageway.

I'll take conversation from which there is a chance to learn something in preference to the details in a news column nearly any time. For a few minutes the talk was about Sir Isaac Newton's books. Macmillan told how Newton's copy of Euclid had been picked up for a shilling when it was worth hundreds of dollars. All book collectors gloat over bargains. I remembered that Thomas Jefferson considered Newton one of the three most "remarkable men of the world," and how Jefferson's own library became the foundation for the great Congressional Library at Washington.

But a dog always has his day among strangers. This one in our compartment was a very affectionate-natured and modest little dog. It came over to my feet and put its head on my knee, remaining as still as a cuddled-up child. Macmillan said that was a compliment to me, and that it is a good sign when a dog likes a man. I asked him if he had ever read O. Henry's "Theory and the Hound." He could not recall that particular story, though, like many other Englishmen, he places O. Henry at the top of storytellers. The "theory," I reminded him, is that a man who is kind to dogs is a brute to women, which theory O. Henry's sheriff used to identify a wife-torturer for whom he took extradition papers to Central America.

After the conversation got this far, the dark, heavy-set man standing in the door could restrain himself no longer. He did not know any of us and no one of us knew him. He told about a sheep dog his father used to own that somebody stole. Two weeks later a constable reported a strange dog in a farmer's kennel twelve miles away. The dark man, just a boy at the time, was sent to identify it. He found the dog apparently satisfied with his new home; it made no demonstration when it saw the newly arrived member of its old family.

"Yes, that is our sheep dog," the boy said.

"You are mistaken. That is my dog," the farmer said.

"Call him and let's see if he knows you," the constable said.

The farmer said, "Here, Judge, here!"

The dog paid no attention to him.

"Now, you call him," the constable said to the boy.

"Prince, come here," the boy called.

Prince arose and walked over to the boy.

"Take him home," the constable said.

This reminded Macmillan of a case in the London courts some time ago. Two women were claiming a particular dog, and the claimants were brought before a judge who thought he would play Solomon. He called upon the first woman to demonstrate the dog's attachment to her. When she called it, it jumped up into her lap and showed itself very much pleased. The second woman was asked to show how well the dog knew her. It jumped up into her lap and made strong demonstrations of affection. Then while the judge was pondering, it jumped up on the table in front of the clerk and tried to kiss him. The judge had to call for further evidence.

The dark heavy-set man at the door pulled in a suitcase and sat on it. He had just started on dog stories. I had to tell about Alf Robinson of Live Oak County and his horse. It was soon after the Civil War and the Texas border country was the hunting ground for horse thieves. Some of them, Mexicans, stole the bay horse that Alf Robinson had ridden for four years in the Confederate Army and brought home after his discharge. About three years later he met a drove of horses trailing north from the Rio Grande and recognized in it his beloved bay. The owner of the herd declared that the horse Alf Robinson pointed out was an outlaw and called attention to the Mexican brand on him. I will not detail the whole story here. In the end after the horses had been corralled and the bay had been roped by a vaquero and had defied him, he ran snorting to the side of his lawful master, who had quietly called him.

The dark man waited patiently until I had finished my longish narrative. Then he leaped into an account of a dog that used to get on a bus at a certain place nearly every day, put a passenger off the front seat, take it himself, ride to a village where a member of his master's family lived, and get off. Nobody ever seemed to resent this dog's taking a front seat. The bus people were all proud of the dog as a privileged character and didn't try to charge him a fare.

A man who had sat silent up to now piped up and told how a dog got shoved off the platform at a tube station in London, how an oncoming train about to run over the dog stopped, how a trainman got down on the tracks to rescue the dog but had to chase him, thus forcing another train to stop, and how a network of underground trains was brought to a standstill before the bewildered dog was finally rescued.

The dark man introduced a dog that always knows when the day comes to set the clock back in summer and thus the hour of tea — and of his tidbit — is changed. And this brought Macmillan to his cat.

"I've been having to explain to my cat," he said, "about the scarcity of meat. 'See here,' I said to him the other evening at the dinner table, 'you are carnivorous by nature. Nobody could blame you for wanting meat. But listen, haven't you been paying some attention to Lord Woolton over the radio? He's Minister of Food, you know. Nobody can keep from being impressed by his figures on the great potato crop of England. He's always telling us how nour- ishing potatoes are and how we'll be strong and healthy eating them even if we do go short on meat. Really, sir, I feel embarrassed at calling your attention to the matter, but you must have noticed the meat shortage. Honestly, as a patriot, don't you think you might take a potato once a day? I wouldn't suggest that you eat potatoes three times a day, as so many of us do, but after all, you're one of us, you know. The Minister of Food is depending on all of us.' "

Macmillan averred that the cat became terribly serious while listening to this explanation, even seemed embar- rassed. "Then," he said, "I offered my cat a boiled potato off the table. He looked at it, he looked at me. He tasted the potato, looked at me again. I told him to keep on eat- ing, and now he eats a potato for dinner every evening."

By now we were halfway and more to London. Every- body in the compartment felt jolly. . . . I thought of a proverb that a Mexican gave to me while four of us were riding horseback over a mountain trail in Durango one winter day. We had all been talking and the three Mexi- cans had been singing about Pancho Villa and other heroes in their language and I had been trying to comply with "Sam Bass" and "When the Roll Is Called up Yonder" in my language. I had hardly noticed that darkness was falling until I saw a light ahead, down the mountain.

"It is from the hacienda," the Mexican said.

"The ride has seemed very short," I said. We had been riding since noon.

"Yes," the Mexican said, "as the saying goes, 'With singing the road is shortened.'" . . .

Now, in the train up to London, I had not noticed, until we drew to a halt at a station, that a slow, purposeless drizzle was falling from skies so low that you might have punched them with a fishing pole.

Our train was a long one, and the station platform was long too. It was peopled with American soldiers, under helmets and with full equipment in regulation khaki sacks. There were evidently some cars on the train reserved for them, but the group of soldiers outside our window did not know where the cars were located. Their tonic voices came in to us.

"My tin's getting wet."

"Paint won't rust."

"Boys, I know you love this place, but come on. Get hustling. This way."

Still the men in uniforms did not shift.

"I hear a voice I recognize," I said.

"Native woodnotes wild," Macmillan smiled.

"Well, I ain't got nuthin' bothering me," a hearty voice sang out, and the figures in the drizzle swung the sacks to shoulders and began moving towards another car. The girl with the little dog looked so bright that the drizzle faded out, and before another pipe could be smoked we were in London town. Maybe an Englishman won't al-

ways break the ice first, but when it is broken he will swim
like a leviathan.

One morning I got into a compartment in London with
a party of three oldish women and a thoroughly old man
going to a funeral. They began breakfasting on meat pies
and buns, which they wanted me to share, but I had had
my coffee early. The old fellow was a kind of pet lion
among the ladies and made several remarks that brought
forth admiring reproaches. One of the women was his wife,
and she gave a disquisition on his sleeping habits. He did
not blame the American soldiers for drinking up pub
beer. I had just read an ancient pamphlet undertaking to
prove that the word "merrie" as applied to England and
nightingales originally meant "cheerful." I reflected — and
many other encounters have confirmed the reflection — that
while English people may not be so gay as they were when
Queen Elizabeth wanted to dance around the Maypole,
they are constitutionally cheerful.

While I was standing one day on the station platform
at Cambridge, a young lady whom I had met several times
with an admiring collegian saluted me. She was going to
London to train in a company of actors expecting to tour
British camps in France. Her sister, with her, was going
to Oxford by way of London. Contrary to my custom, I
had bought a first-class ticket, for I knew the train would
be crowded and I was not ambitious to stand. The young
ladies had only third-class tickets. After they found all
seats occupied in a third-class coach, they came back into
the first class, and we all managed to sit in the same compartment.

In it was a very handsomely groomed handsome gentleman — dark, about forty years old, his features all alert,
nothing garish about him. At first he took no part in our
talk. In the compartment were a British soldier also and
a woman of habitual quietness. Presently the collector of
tickets came around. He gave the two young women and
the soldier the choice of paying three shillings each extra
fare or going back into a third-class coach, where he said
there were seats. As he left, the handsome gentleman got
up and had a word with him in the aisle. Returning, he
said that he doubted if the collector would come back,
and advised the young people to keep their seats. But in
about five minutes the collector did come back. He was
not to be argued with. Then the handsome gentleman said,
"I will pay the extra fares." He pulled out a wallet of five-
pound notes. The collector could not make change. "You
will have to go," he said, looking at the third-class fares.
"Maybe I can find something smaller," the handsome gentleman said. He reached into his trousers' pocket and pulled
out a roll of pound notes big enough to choke a cow. The
collector took out nine shillings, gave a receipt, and now
we were all settled and all acquainted. Soon the handsome
gentleman opened his satchel and produced three pears,
each wrapped in tissue paper, as large as I have ever seen.
To each of the three ladies he presented one. He had one
left, he explained, when they protested. The drift of his
talk indicated that he was a race-horse man; I am sure that
he had met good luck — after using good judgment — on
the races at Newmarket the day before. At the London
station he lugged a very heavy suitcase, while I lugged

another, down into the tube for the young ladies, said good-
by, and that is all about him.

After two hours' ride on a train to Bristol that evening —
the papers all read, and all that I wanted of a book — I
struck up talk with a fellow passenger. She was interested
in Laurence Housman's writings and in the intellectual
curiosity of her little girl at home. "What is God's other
name?" the little girl had asked. "God what?" Again,
"When Jesus was a little boy did his nose run?" Also,
"Do angels have engines in them? . . . They don't? Then
how do angels fly?"

No, if I want to talk I do not find it the least difficult
to talk to people in England, on trains or elsewhere. The
last time honest Jim Standefer, a sergeant from Bosque
County, Texas, came to see me he was telling me about
his trip on the train. The compartment was already full,
he said, when a man, woman and five-year-old boy came
into it. He gave his seat to the woman. After a while
the boy began whining for a drink of water, but the compartment was one of the kind that you can't get out of
except at a station and that has no connection with water
intake or outlet. Jim had an army issue of carbohydrates
in his pockets — sweets. He gave them to the kid, and
tears turned to laughter. He had a package wrapped up
in the colored comics of a Philadelphia paper that one
of his crew gets. He unfolded the paper and gave it to
the kid, but it did not interest him as much as it interested
the whole compartment of grown people. They passed
it around among themselves, commenting and asking questions, and by the time the train reached Cambridge they

were all talking to each other. As Jim said, if some spark like that had not been struck among them, they would probably not have said a word the whole distance. I've noticed many times that the English don't always rely on Americans for sparks.

CHAPTER IV
In Winter's Darkness

I'M ALWAYS wanting something," General Robert E. Lee said. Not power, or fame, or money, or love, or a plantation with darkies to wait on him; nor grandchildren to play in the beard whitened by Gettysburg and the Wilderness. Not songs. He wasn't a man to talk about himself; he had almost no concern for his own welfare, but one can imagine that the dim quaver of a soldier's song marking where a campfire had died down on a summer night made him feel more poignantly and more vaguely the undefined want of that undefined "something." It was the kind of something that Cyclone Denton used to say he was always hunting. Not many know Cyclone Denton. Generous-souled John Rosser of Dallas helped Cyclone Denton print his reminiscences. Cyclone said, "It seems like I have always been hunting for something that I didn't know what it was."

I

It is as dark as the inside of a cow here in the city of Cambridge. In London it is as dark as a burglar's pocket.

In many another place in England it is as dark as the back corner of a bear's den. If glass were not so fragile, I'd take a jar outside and let a sample of the fog settle into it and send it home. The fog hereabouts comes up from the Fens, they say — the Fens that the Romans were building a road across two thousand years ago. The trains are creeping through the fog hours late. Last night the buses all stopped running. I thought about the drivers of the army trucks and cars forever on the move, shifting between east and west, north and south, as ceaselessly, it seems, as the currents of air everlastingly unstabilized between frigid and torrid. The dark is thicker tonight than it was last night. Maybe it is too thick to carry the sound of motors in the sky. At least, I have not noticed the throb of a plane for hours.

But the dark never gets heavy enough to keep people inside. I step out on the street and, except in the puddle of light made by my own torch (flashlight as called elsewhere), I can distinguish nothing. I do see coming and going brief dots of other torches, no stronger or more constant than the glowing of lightning bugs in a starlit valley. The toy lights on bicycles are more constant; if it were not for the tinkling of the cyclist bells, you'd think the lights were another kind of firefly. Any automobile daring the darkness is as dim as the bicycle light — and nearly as slow in its progress. No matter how dark the night, the automobile driver cannot brighten his lights by a candle-power.

But it is not lights or absence of lights in the darkness that strikes one; it is the sounds from human feet and

human voices. Especially feet. Boots, boots, boots, marching all together. I linger to let five or six voices and pairs of
feet pass me. They are out in the middle of the narrow
street, keeping step and keeping time. The voices and the
firm but lightsome foot-plantings are of young women.
They are singing a song about something far away. It is
a love song with sadness in it — the only kind of love songs
that ever were or ever will be beautiful. From the step, step,
step and from half of a glimpse of a swinging arm as the
voices pass me, I know that they belong to military women.
There are other foot-sounds without voices. Many of them.
Some timid and groping; most of them direct. Hardly
any pedestrian keeps his torch burning constantly. Every
one must save his batteries. There are voices now and
then that seem to be without feet. The Americans sometimes
have louder voices, not always. Passing the mouth of a side
street, I hear down it, in the direction of The Blue Boar,

Where the deer and the antelope play.

For every audible voice, there seem to be dozens of audible feet. Now there is silence, broken only by my own
steps. Presently I hear another person's steps. I don't want
to flash my light. My eyes are accommodated to the dark,
and a light will unfocus them. I guess the other person feels
the same way, or maybe he does not have a light to flash, or
maybe he likes the mysteries of darkness. He is not far
away and we both stop at the same time, each to try to
locate the other and prevent a collision. We pass without
grazing. Now there is another wave of foot-beats. The
lightning bugs are again in the air.

I know which direction I am walking, but I don't know why or to where. I am just walking. I am looking for something, I guess. There is a kind of hunger inside of me for something. I don't know what it is. I wouldn't find it in any club or home. I wouldn't find it in a pub. I wouldn't find it in a book back in my room. I can't think of any place on earth where I might find it right now. True, it would be soothing to sit by a fire of mesquite wood, behind a natural windbreak, away out in the big pasture country, and watch the Great Dipper swing; yet that is not what I want. I wonder if all the people who are thumping their feet on the cement sidewalks and the paved street know where they are going, know why they are going, know what they want. I don't think so.

The politicians always try to tell them what they want — something cheap that can be bought with dollars. One politician has tried to tell them that what they want is rubber, another that it is gasoline, another that it is uncontrolled prices on wheat. But rubber never made anybody happy. The cheaper a politician is the cheaper the want is that he imagines other people feel and that he tries to little-ize them into crying for. But no all-day sucker ever lasted over twenty minutes. No child, much less an adult, ever found an all-day sucker that filled his wants.

Steps, steps, steps in the dark going somewhere. Voices in the dark saying something. "I'm always wanting something," General Lee said — said just once, and went on his marble way. When I was a very young man I found a sentence in Emerson that puzzled me then and awes me now. "Young man, be careful what you want, for you will

surely get it." Surely, I thought, life cannot be so simple
as that. Years of experience and observation have taught me
that Emerson was — and is — absolutely and literally right.
We haven't all got as much as we wanted of whatever it is
we wanted; many have got too much of it, a sickening,
dreary surfeit of it; all have got the kind, the quality, of
thing they wanted.

For months now I have done little but read the history
of my country — thousands of pages. I have been struck
with how through the repeated decades of American history the people have got what they wanted. In the beginning they were greatly concerned with "the rights of
man" and with not only freedom but enlightenment. They
got noble Washington, great and thoughtful Jefferson,
righteous and unyielding old John Quincy Adams for
their leaders. A hundred years went on, and the people
were all mad for "normalcy." Democracy consisted no
longer in the "unalienable rights" of man to "life, liberty
and the pursuit of happiness," but in having things. The
American way of life became the business way of life. And
the people got as their leader a business man — Warren G.
Harding, as sorry and as muddleheaded a character as ever
occupied the sorriest throne of the most rundown prin-
cipality of Europe.

In the days of Washington and Jefferson and on through
the years till the Civil War, the ambition of able — and
many not able — young lawyers was to be a United States
senator and to help in a grand way to govern their country.
By the time big business took over government, the usual
ambition of a bright young lawyer became, as it still is, to

get himself retained by some corporation. The desire to serve his country had changed to a desire to sell his soul to a rich corporation, which is for legal purposes a "person," but which, morally, is without conscience or humanity. And the young lawyers of each age got what they wanted. Not all of the first age could be John Randolphs or Websters, or all in the second age draw salaries from Standard Oil, but all got the kind of thing they wanted to get.

I wonder why people say "as dark as Egypt." Egypt connects with Moses. "Where was Moses when the light went out? Sitting in the window with his shirttail out." Egypt can't be any darker than this. It's getting quite late now, and footfalls, voices, fog-dimmed glowworm lights, have become very sparse. I am in one of the narrow crooked little streets, laid out perhaps by cranes wading a trail through the Fens back in the Middle Ages. I still don't know what I'm wanting, but I'm going back to my rooms. The buildings lining this street are only three or four stories high but it is so narrow that they make it like a little canyon. The least noise in it echoes, the sound cushioned by the fog. I'm walking soft myself, and then I hear footfalls. I don't know whether to keep left or take right; nobody else who walks in the blackout knows, but the earth-treader approaching me evidently has no feelings of hesitation. His shoes are heavy — soldier shoes probably. He's busting along. I flash my torch, just for a few seconds so's not to dis-focus my night-horse eyes. The soldier puts on the brakes.

"Say," he said, "how do you git to the Bull Hotel from here?"

I told him. The Bull Hotel is run for American soldiers by the American Red Cross.

"You live in this country?" the soldier in the dark asked — after my speech had betrayed me. I knew what he was coming to. I had noted his accents also.

"Well," I replied, "I'm living here right now."

"How long you been here?"

"Oh, two or three months."

"Where'd you come from?"

"United States."

"What part?"

"Southern."

"What state?"

"Texas."

"I knew it, I knew it, soon as I heard your voice. What place in Texas?"

"Austin."

"My name's Ellis and I live in Rockdale, just sixty miles from Austin. Ever there?"

"Well, I've been through Rockdale lots of times. Once I went there to see a friend."

"Who?"

"George Sessions Perry."

"Gee! Everybody in Rockdale knows George Sessions Perry. He wrote a novel about Texas."

In a more confidential tone: "What you think about this country?"

"What do you think about it?"

"Well, the people are all right."

"Yes, the people are all right." It was my time to ask a question. "Do you know W. T. Pearson of Rockdale?

He's a sergeant over here. I saw him last week. He's using George Sessions Perry's book on Texas for the Bible."

"Sure I know Pearson. What'd you say your name was?"

I really had not said.

The soldier in the dark went on. "Well, just think. I ask a stranger here in this blackout how to find the Bull Hotel, and the stranger turns out to be a neighbor in Texas, and he knows two people in Rockdale. I guess I better get on now and sleep a little. Strange though, ain't it?"

"Sort of strange."

"Good night."

"Good night, Ellis. Good luck!"

I like real soldiers. I like ships that pass in the blacked-out night. Now I seem to know better what it is I am wanting.

2

When I go to London — and I can never go there often enough or stay long enough — I have a home. It is a fine old house with fifty bedrooms, dining room, an extensive library rich in American as well as English books, and other graces and facilities owned and operated by the English-Speaking Union. Dartmouth House, it is called, and it is one of several such clubs that extend hospitality to Americans in this country. I pay for my room, very difficult to get at any hotel, and for my meals, at moderate prices. Above all, I get at the Dartmouth House something that money does not buy.

I have heard numerous air-raid warnings, but it was in Dartmouth House in London that for the first time I heard the anti-aircraft guns go into action, saw the pyrotechnics in the sky. I thought of the story of the understating Englishman. "Is that thunder?" he exclaimed. "No," replied another Englishman, "it's German bombs." "Good. I was afraid it was going to rain."

The night turned absolutely clear and about three hours after the raid was over, I saw something in the sky to remember. The stars were not so bright as in Texas, but they spangled the whole welkin and seemed to me as "beautiful and fair" as ever were "waters on a starry night." I stood alone in Green Park in the heart of London; there were no passers-by, though it was only ten o'clock. Not a hundred yards away a searchlight that seemed to be more powerful than scores of other searchlights casting rays from all parts of the vast city was throwing its beam across the spaces. The Great Hunter hunted low down in the east, and the North Star stood much higher than it stands at home. It was a great comfort to feel myself correctly oriented, my poor instinct for direction coinciding with the great fact of polarity declared by the heavens. Tonight I was not *norteado* (northed), as the vaqueros say when a man is lost.

Then, far away, somewhat west of north, I saw the giant beam from the searchlight leading a silver plane across the sky, over London. Other beams converged on the plane until there were eighteen or nineteen focused on it at one time. It was so high up that I did not hear its motors, or it was so beautiful that I forgot to listen. It was manifestly one of our planes. It flew as easy, as light, as innocent, as bright as the white dove of peace. The great soft bands of brightened air seemed to be caressing and guiding the lovely ship as if it were some feather-wafted nursling of the sky. Had any enemy come into those serene spaces, they would have exploded into avalanches of fury and destruction. But there was no enemy now. A little way off the ruins of bombed walls had been turned by the shadows of night into a soft dream. And the airy sliver of brightness up there in the apex of the searchlight beams moved on as softly as a feather is wafted downward from an eagle in its flight. It moved clear across the sky, and the beams seemed to have put it to bed, when the giant of all the searchlights made another band into the north and played on another plane. "You are one of our children, one of ours," the beams seemed to say, as thick and fast they converged on this new nursling. Almost immediately another plane was in another beam and then in a cluster of beams. Then a third plane became a center of light-play, while the other two were still being escorted, the beams coming up so thickly that all three planes had, each for itself, full attention.

It would be something to capture and put down for others to comprehend the feelings of the men and women who work the searchlights in London and with beams fondle their own R.A.F. nurslings. By coincidence, just one night after the spectacle I have described, I had a fractional insight into the feelings. One of the first deeds I performed after arriving in England was to go to Thetford, the birth-place of that English-American-French fighter for freedom, Tom Paine, and help the 388th Bomber Group present a commemorative plaque to the town's citizens. This group had named one of their Flying Fortresses *Tom Paine*, and on the grim steel beneath the name painted one of Paine's piercing sentences: "TYRANNY, LIKE HELL, IS NOT EASILY CONQUERED." After exploring the insides of the Fortress, talking with pilot and gunners and seeing the ground crew shoving keepsakes for Germany into her racks, I came to feel that the whole outfit, men and machines, would de-fend "The Rights of Man" till hell froze over, and a little while on the ice — which would be long enough to satisfy nervous Tom Paine himself. Also, I came to have a very personal feeling for that particular fort of the air.

While I stood in the London park watching the lovely ships in the light beams, saying to myself as each shining one came into view, "It's one of ours," I remembered that other one of ours to which I stand as a kind of godfather. The very next night while prowling along Piccadilly, I halted at a very small, very dimly lit sign, "Restaurant." I had passed two or three other signs of the same character. Going through a door and then through a curtain, I came into a cheerfully lighted place of food smells. It was small-ish and had few eaters. At one table I passed three Ameri-can uniforms, sergeant stripes on two of them. The face of the third man came to me as a memory out of somewhere. He did not look at me, and I could not place him. I sat with my back to him and was no longer conscious of him when I suddenly realized that he was standing beside me and calling my name. He was the Red Cross man of the 388th Bomber Group.

He and other men from his base had come to London to give a pattern of skits and songs, nearly all satirical, at one of the American army centers. We talked about the *Tom Paine*. It had just completed its twentieth sortie, not been shot up "much," all its crew sound and all of them believing in Tom Paine as strongly as Indian-minded Sam Houston believed in ravens. While we waited for the show to start, I sat down and wrote a Christmas letter to the lads, ground and air, of the *Tom Paine* — one of ours for certain.

CHAPTER V
Kind Hearts

CHRISTMAS always makes me more sure of one thing in this fluctuating world than of anything else. That is, that kind hearts are the best thing in the world; that

> Kind hearts are more than coronets,
> And simple faith than Norman blood.

And this Christmas of 1943, in England, far away from my own home, I have been made more sure of that fact than ever. Here it is three days after Christmas and the church bells are still ringing in my ears and in my heart. Not that there was much literal ringing of church bells — except for the beautiful ones selected for broadcasting. For four Christmases now they have not rung out all over the land on Christmas morning as they are wont to ring out in normal times. They have not rung because it was agreed early in the war that the ringing of the church bells would be an alarm against the enemy. Most people think they will ring twice during the coming year as they have never rung before — once to announce victory over the Germans, and again next Christmas to announce the coming peace over the world and the coming growth of good will towards all men. Back in the dark ages it was a belief that if human blood was put into molten metal, the tone of the bell cast from it would be sweeter. If human blood does make the bell tone sweeter, then the ringing on that coming Christmas, when peace is again pealed out, will be sweeter than ever in all history men and women and children have heard it.

There is one thing sweeter than a beautiful bell though, and that is the Christmas wish of some sincere person who gives you the wish out of his heart and not merely out of convention. Five days before Christmas General Pleas B. Rogers, son of Captain J. H. Rogers of the Texas Rangers, now in command of all the vast and diversified American operations over the 750 square miles of the "Central Base Section" called London, was showing me some of the activities of his area. It was late night when his car drove up to the terminus of one branch of the city's wonderful underground railway system. The subways are bored through clay more than one hundred and thirty feet under the street surface, and bombs have never penetrated to them. In certain places borings intended for extension of the electric-run underground railways have been turned into shelters against air raids and are fitted up with beds and other necessary appointments.

The tube shelter where General Rogers took me has eight hundred beds reserved for American service men on leave. The service men are taken there on nights when too many of them have crowded into London for the Red Cross hostels, the always-crowded hotels and other sleeping places to accommodate. There they are given clean

sheets and blankets and, one hundred and thirty feet underground, sleep in air as pure as that on top of Pike's Peak.
Technicians showed us the air-conditioning machinery, and
it is, I am sure, as improved as exists anywhere on earth,
arranged to switch to alternate currents and reserves of
electricity that not all the German bombs extant could
throw out of service.

After we had inspected the cathedral-like corridors of
beds, the store rooms, the plumbing and the machinery, the
manager of this subterranean refuge led us into a side room
where we were surprised to find upwards of twenty volunteer workers. More than half of them were women; the
men were all beyond the age of military service. Both men
and women were of what is generally called "the working class," though that class now includes virtually everybody in the United Kingdom. These people are up at daylight to work; they work long hours; and at night they
serve as air wardens and attendants in the underground
hostel. It is often nearer daylight than midnight before the
last soldier has been bedded down. It was up to General
Rogers to say something to the workers. He asserts that
he is not a public speaker, but he made one of the best
short speeches I have ever heard any man make. He told
that little group of volunteers, respect for his rank and
kindness of heart written all over their features, that he
was speaking for families everywhere in America when
he thanked them for the hospitality they show nightly to
American boys. He told them that he had been in England
a long time now, and that he had come to appreciate how
their spirit represents the whole English spirit. I have heard

him in private talk say the same sort of thing more than once.

Well, we were leaving when two very plain women sitting knitting while they waited for a call, near the door, said, almost together, "Happy Christmas to you both."

I cannot tell why or how, so deep down there in the caverns of refuge, not only against German destruction but for American boys, those words came home to me. I suppose it was because they were so sincerely meant. The good natural things of this old world never grow stale — like sunrises, moonlight, the blue of bluebonnets in the spring, the startled cry of the killdee or curlew from its ground perch, the whistling of a man on horseback riding along a trail at night, the mist rising over the water on a winter morning, the cuddling down of a child to sleep, the feel of a loved woman's hand on a fevered forehead, the voice of a comrade who cares after he has not seen you for a long time or when he is telling you good-by for what may be forever. Like a quiet bell, away off on a Sunday morning, I keep hearing the "Happy Christmas" of those two kindly featured, plainly dressed working women down in the caverns so deep under the streets of London.

In the college hall where I have rooms in Cambridge, two other plain women, designated as "bed-makers," bring in coal, make the coal fires, scrub the hearths, draw the water, draw back the black blackout curtains, make the beds, change the linen and otherwise administer to us gentlemen. Two weeks ago, they both took at the same time the mild but devastating form of influenza that has been sweeping the country. Neither one quit work, however.

"You see, sir," one of them explained to me, "we could not let each other down." One of them has three children at home and a husband in the army. The other one has a boy in the R.A.F. and other children, and for years now she has had two soldiers quartered in her house. She gets up a long while before daylight and gives those two soldiers and her family breakfast and gets to college in time to wake some of her charges up for breakfast there. They both do their own washing, cooking and other housework. It was "as good as a church service," as good as the blessing of a father in a play, when these two good women wished me "A Happy Christmas, sir."

"And how are you going to spend Christmas?" I asked a waiter of the dining hall. "It will be mostly memories this year," he replied with a certain dignity, "but that should sustain us until victory. A Happy Christmas to you, sir!"

I had several invitations to Christmas dinner — and nobody who invited me had anything to spare. In the afternoon about teatime I called at a home that has been open to me on several occasions. These people had been unable to get "a bird" for Christmas, but they and their neighbors were combining on a rooster that the neighbors procured weeks back and began feeding in a way supposed to tenderize the meat. My host for Christmas dinner is the manager of a seven-hundred-acre farm owned by Cambridge University. A practical scientist, he is one of the best-known agriculturalists in England. His name is W. S. Mansfield. We had a turkey. There were eight of us, including a doctor and his wife, who is a Hollander; they both escaped from Holland a little ahead of the Germans.

Mansfield poured wine in wine glasses on the table. Good wine has become as scarce as "birds" and razor blades. "We are going to have some toasts," he said. Twice during the meal he repeated the words. I took them as a warning against drinking down all the wine. After the plum pudding, than which nothing is more English or more satisfying to my mind, taste and stomach, Mansfield arose and we did likewise. "Ladies and gentlemen," he said, "to His Majesty the King!" We raised our glasses, repeated the words and sat down.

Again Mansfield rose, we following. "Ladies and gentlemen," he said, "to her Highness, the Queen of Holland, and to our guest, Mrs. Laird!" We raised glasses, looked to the lady from Holland, and repeated the words.

A third time Mansfield arose. "Ladies and gentlemen, to the President of the United States of America and to our guest, Professor Dobie!"

These were emphatically not mere forms. I don't know what I said when I was called on for "speech, speech" at the conclusion of the last toast. It was stumbling, I know, and I know also that it was not mere form. The sincere kindheartedness of these people will abide with me as long as my ears remain open to hear Christmas greetings and Christmas bells.

Then we had one more toast that, according to tradition, must have been drunk in thousands of places on this Day of Remembrance by these island people whose destiny and whose pride it has been for a thousand years to go over the seas. "Ladies and gentlemen, here's to our wives and sweethearts, to absent friends and to ships upon the sea!"

When Dickens wrote his *Christmas Carol* he was but reflecting Bob Cratchit's countrymen — and "God bless us every one." I knew this kindheartedness long ago, before I had seen the Atlantic Ocean. I knew it from reading in Charles Lamb about Jem White, who used to give the chimney sweepers such a dinner. I knew it from Washington Irving's account of "Christmas at Bracebridge Hall." I knew it from a thousand printed sources. I was not looking for the old days of great bounty, about which the books tell. There is no such physical bounty anywhere in war-worn, war-weary, war-rationed England now. But it has been a great experience to meet the old-time bounty of kindheartedness.

The English people do not exchange so many Christmas cards so promiscuously as we in America do. Their exchanges are largely between friends and do not generally include mere acquaintances. Their Christmas cards do not seem to be used much as political and commercial reminders. The cards have Christmas tones, the jazz quality being almost altogether absent. Every home puts its Christmas cards up on mantelpieces, bookcases, tables, shelves, so that they make a bright and varied display.

On the afternoon of Christmas Eve I went to hear the carols in King's College Chapel, the singing of them by the Chapel choirboys being famous, through the radio, all over the British Commonwealth of Nations. After I came back, the porter at the gate of my college asked me how I enjoyed them. "I always used to go and sit away back so that the singing would come to me through the long spaces," he said. "Happy Christmas, sir!" Always, day and night, a man is on duty in the porter's lodge. Everybody must pass it going in or out of the college. I like to step in and pass words with the porters. They have a radio and sometimes I pause to listen with them to the news and to beautiful music. They read as many newspapers as the dons and are as well-informed on public affairs. Frequently I see one reading a book between calls. However humble their work, they are as intelligent and informed as they are civil and kindhearted. One of them was telling me Christmas morning about the church bells in his native village of Grantchester. That afternoon I walked to it, two miles through fields and meadows along a macadamized walk that threads through half a dozen turnstiles. I asked my companion who paved that walk.

"Why," he said, "the public has always had a right to walk through these fields. About two hundred years ago two Fellows of Cambridge used to be very fond of walking this way, but they didn't like the mud. They must have enjoyed the idea of other people walking this way too. When they died they left a fund in trust to be spent on making and maintaining a hard-surfaced walk. There will always be a good walk here, I suppose." This kind of regard for posterity and the graces of life is civilization.

A Christmas will come when the bells of Grantchester church and the bells of all the churches in England, which is churched as few other lands are churched, will be ringing out peace. I am absolutely certain that for every part of the world, America included, the perpetuation of that peace depends on an Anglo-American alliance with other countries. What a decent world it could so easily be if public spokesmen, instead of stirring up the people to distrust and to shortsighted grasping, would allow the natural goodness in human hearts on both sides of the Atlantic to operate. The kind of people we can trust humanly are the kind of people we can trust governmentally.

CHAPTER VI
English Conservatism

Politically, a conservative is generally regarded as a person entrenched in privileges that he considers, justifiably or not, as rights. "I do not want revolution," the Manhattan burgher said in 1776. "I have windows in my house." There is a continent of difference between a reactionary, or conservative, who opposes change because he thinks change will curtail his material benefits and a reactionary, or conservative, who opposes change because he is too much in love with things as they are to have them altered, even to his own material advantage. An Englishman reared on a large country estate was telling me how about forty years ago his father stood adamant against the introduction of a bathtub with running water into the house. He preferred his bath in a tin kept under his own bed, filled by a servant, to a bath in any kind of tub that other people might use. He preferred, in other words, what he was used to. His wife and children finally won the battle. You can set such a man down as stubborn, hopelessly set in his ways; but he is not trying to keep other people down in order to keep himself up. This kind of conservative will stand in his own light more than in that of other people. He would really be willing to pay more taxes in order to be allowed to go his old ways. He is the type that John

Locke had in mind when he wrote: "New opinions are always suspected, and usually opposed, without any other reason but because they are not already common." In "The Old Squire," Wilfrid Scawen Blunt has compacted the very essence of the type.

> I like the hunting of the hare
> Better than that of the fox;
> I like the joyous morning air,
> And the crowing of the cocks. . . .
>
> The beagles at my horse-heels trot,
> In silence after me;
> There's Ruby, Roger, Diamond, Dot,
> Old Slut and Margery, —
>
> A score of names well used, and dear,
> The names my childhood knew;
> The horn with which I rouse their cheer
> Is the horn my father blew.
>
> I like the hunting of the hare
> Better than that of the fox;
> The new world still is all less fair
> Than the old world it mocks.
>
> I covet not a wider range
> Than these dear manors give;
> I take my pleasures without change,
> And as I lived I live. . . .
>
> I know my quarries every one,
> The meuse where she sits low;
> The road she chose to-day was run
> A hundred years ago. . . .

I like the hunting of the hare;
   It brings me, day by day,
The memory of old days as fair,
   With dead men passed away.

To these, as homeward still I ply
   And pass the churchyard gate,
Where all are laid as I must lie,
   I stop and raise my hat.

I like the hunting of the hare;
   New sports I hold in scorn.
I like to be as my fathers were,
   In the days ere I was born.

I

As I write, newspaper columns are clattering with the
clashes of opinions — and of interests — over the proposal
of an electric supply company to build a $16,000,000 power
plant near the ancient city of Durham — which people in
England associate more with its castle and cathedral than
with the red cattle and roll-your-own tobacco that to
many Americans afford the name's only connection. After
publication of the fact that the company had received a
license from the Durham County Council to build, a rash
of protests broke out against what is characterized as a
defilement of the view of cathedral and castle, especially
from the railroad. The power plant would be between the
railroad and the center of the city. Members of the Society

for the Protection of Ancient Buildings became particularly vocal. The Bishop of Durham and other churchmen raised their voices high.

In reply a spokesman for the Durham County Council said: —

"Under the heading 'Durham from the Railway,' *The Times* has unwittingly crystallised the national attitude of the past twenty years towards Durham and similar distressed areas. During this period of localized distress, when governments shirked their national as well as international responsibilities, the title 'Distressed Area' came to signify those areas to be avoided if possible, or if some contact was unavoidable, to be viewed with impersonal interest from the railway when passing from one more fortunate district to another.

"The view of Durham from the railway is, without doubt, particularly beautiful, especially if one chooses not to see the slum clearance areas that intervene. It seems that the conscience of the nation, and indeed of the Church, is more easily stirred by the prospect that this view may be marred than it was by the poverty and despair which before the war ruined the lives of the country's inhabitants and which the project will do something to redress. Let the proposed site be examined. If, however, in the opinion of experts, it is the only proper site, this council will be prepared to put the claims of the people to a life of economic security above the claims of those critics who view Durham from the railway or indeed from the Cathedral and Castle."

*　　*　　*

After this blast, the critics turned to a consideration of the evils of manufacturing architecture in general, the suffering in health and comfort due to "emissions from chimneys and cooling towers," the threats looming ahead to Lincoln Cathedral, even to Loch Lomond in Scotland, and to other beauties of nature and art unless the Ministry of Town and Country Planning intervenes.

It seems a case in which everybody is right, including the capitalists who are to erect the Durham power plant. If the advantageous site — advantageous because of the lay of the land next to accessible water — is changed, it will not do as much material good to as many people as it might have done. If the selected site is built on, the cathedral and castle, existing mostly to be looked at, will shrink as pictures. England simply is not big enough to comprehend the century of the common man and at the same time to maintain the centuries of the feudal lord. Personally I had rather spend the six English winter months in a comfortably heated and cheerfully lighted barn than have to endure them shivering in the sunless darkness, the clinging dampness and the stony, marrow-sucking coldness of any majestic cathedral or proud castle that the serf-treading bishops and lords of the Middle Ages erected. Yet, some say, what is the sense of teaching aesthetic values to children in the common schools while at the same time you destroy the aesthetic?

2

Conservatism is not necessarily reactionary. It may be quite the contrary, though this truism is constantly forgotten by zealous progressives. The *Manchester Guardian* would never be called a reactionary newspaper; it is decidedly conservative and decidedly progressive. In many ways liberalism can depend more consistently on British conservatism than on radicalism. Any haste it makes will certainly be made slowly, but it won't walk backwards and is not likely to trip itself up plunging forward. Danger to human beings dependent on it lies not in the conservatism itself but in its susceptibility to being run over by something progressive only in the physical sense. Sometimes I think that progress is a state of society in which nobody in particular wants to run but everybody must run in order to keep from being run over. The Government was quite conservative that in 1934 established the British Council to promote good relations with foreign countries and to bring the light of British civilization slightly out from under the bushel. One cannot conceive of English cultural propaganda as being fanatical in the manner of Nazi propaganda, which set out to overawe what it could not convert. Conservatism in its best form is a synonym for "modesty of nature."

All statesmen are politicians, though comparatively few politicians are statesmen. Most statesmen have to compromise as politicians in order to effect even the wisest policies of state. I suppose that the reputation of the British for compromising and balancing is based considerably on their way of clinging to the old while admitting, often unwillingly, the new. They have not always been so, but capitalistic conservatives of Britain today seem more willing than their stiff-necked American counterparts to accommodate themselves to the socialistic trends inevitable in society.

The conservatives motivated by taste, particularly taste in architecture, and by "The Old Squire" sentiment for old names, old fields, old ways, are an integral part of the British soil. There is something of the martyr in their resistance to change — often also something of the bull — and a good deal of sheer inertia. When the love for an old hall by a college of dons dooms charwomen to carry coal-scuttles up and slopjars down three flights of stairs, the conservatism has a flavor not idyllic. Yet kitchen help in my college almost struck last winter over the installation of a plate washer. After I had dined with a Foreign Office man in one of the largest clubs of much beclubbed London, we went into the big loungeroom for coffee. A middle-aged woman, black-dressed, brought it, one of her hands bandaged and in a sling supporting the tray. What was the matter with her hand? my host asked. Strain from carrying trays from the kitchen in the basement up to the ground floor, more than fifty round trips every evening, sometimes a hundred. A doctor had advised rest; she could not take off, for there was no one else to carry the trays. At home she had a family in a nine-room house to look after.

"How easy it would be, or would have been, in normal

times," my host commented, "to build a dumb-waiter to carry the trays up and down."

In some of the coal mines of England and Wales miners continue in wretched forms of physical drudgery elsewhere done away with by improved machinery. Yet the miners themselves, it seems, are more averse to new machinery than the mine-owners are. On icy days I have seen women on their knees scrubbing with a hand brush flagstones that could be easily and quickly cleaned with hose and stiff broom. In a country where the Society for the Prevention of Cruelty to Animals is as familiar as the strains of "God Save the King" and as highly regarded for its humaneness as the King is for his kindness, there seems to be no particular sentiment for installing machinery to alleviate human drudgery. No doubt the surplus of population and, consequently, of labor in normal times is partly responsible. Putting the laborer out of a job with a gadget may be more inhumane than keeping the laborer on her knees. Very likely the laborer does not pine to get off her knees. The manager of the Duke of Bedford's estate at Woburn told me that he offered, this year, to install running water in nineteen rent houses at a cost of a few pennies a month, and that only one renter wanted the running water. Some of the others resented the proposal as a landlordly attempt to raise their rents, which are astoundingly cheap. In Mexico if a gringo asks why the hard way of doing a thing is not remedied by an easier way, the invariable answer is, "*No es costumbre.*" Watching a boy in an English field lead a horse hitched to a plow guided by a man, I have imagined that if I asked the man why he did not use plow lines and drive the horse himself, thus saving the use of the boy, he might reply, like the Mexican, "It's not the custom."

The Englishman wants his customs, like his buildings, his machinery, the operations of his institutions, his Church, to stay established. He will pay high for a highly complicated engine designed to get the last ounce of energy out of every drop of oil and every lump of coal, and he will be willing to stand the high cost of maintaining such an engine, rather than install a simpler and cheaper engine of American or German type that wastes a small amount of fuel but costs little to maintain and may be inexpensively discarded for another model to meet changing conditions. Something in him pulls powerfully strong for permanence. Having put up a building, he may add to it and go on adding to it, but he hates to raze it to make way for a structure of entirely new design. The official plan for restreeting the great area demolished by German bombs around Saint Paul's in London is being opposed by conservative architects because the proposed thoroughfares, designed for heavy motor traffic, will not, in the manner of the old alleys too narrow for traffic, invite businessmen to go out bareheaded into the open and transact big business with the casualness of ancient merchants upon the Rialto.

In the parks of London rolls of barbed wire still make the ground hideous and obstruct walking. Most people want the wire taken away and men half idle in military camps could easily take it away; but the Responsibles seem to feel that what is once put should stay put.

"These people," wrote Ambassador Walter Hines Page

to President Wilson in 1914, "are *set*. They naturally shrink from changing anything; they instinctively resent change. A naval man told me that after breech-loading guns were invented, they kept the muzzle-loaders ten years; arguing meantime that no breech-loading guns could possibly be accurate." How did they ever come to start the Machine Age, to make the Industrial Revolution?

It is significant that R.A.F. development of radar to the highest stages of effectiveness in the world has been in a field of science unhampered by tradition, precedents and inherited achievements. In this field caution against discarding the old, lest something good be lost, could not slow down the rush into the new.

"What," Abraham Lincoln asked, "is conservatism? Is it not adherence to the old and tried, against the new and untried?"

> Be not the first by whom the new are tried,
> Nor yet the last to lay the old aside.

Few reform bills have been debated, not alone in Parliament but in print and private conversation, so long, steadily and earnestly as the Education Bill finally made into law in the summer of 1944. The new plan calls for nothing like the French Revolution plan to sweep away all extant gods in order to set up the new Goddess of Reason. It aims to extend education rather than to channel it, to care better for the needs of drudging millions, to project, with modifications, the present multiform system, rather than to melt it all up like so much artwork in gold and silver to be remolded into uniform bars. As the Headmaster of the famous Harrow

School has said: "It is in accordance with variety in the needs and capabilities of children and with the English tradition that within the educational system of the country there should be variety in types of school, in educational methods and freedom to experiment. The vitality of our education depends largely on this variety and freedom." The state is to send poor boys to the so-called public schools, which have so long borne the reputation of being exclusive, but the public schools are to retain their prestige. The state is to support many church secondary schools and by virtue of support to assume stronger direction over them; yet in a way they remain church schools. Compulsory education has long been a fact, but the scholastic age limit has been advanced, and now the need for trained teachers will give women larger representation in the teaching profession than the males have up to the present conceded.

While the scientific age has been accepted in Britain as thoroughly as it has been accepted in America, it has been accepted more critically and less defiantly. Less defiantly, because there is no strong Fundamentalist cult in religion, based on ignorance. More critically, for in accepting science, British conservatism has clung to classical ideals. British universities have not relegated Latin and Greek to the status of Sanskrit as those languages are being relegated by American universities. The Matthew Arnold ideal of infusing the scientific world with sweetness and light, of keeping machinery from becoming Frankenstein by tempering its driver with Hellenism, does not prevail, but it persists.

The most talked-of lecture at Cambridge during my

year's residence has been one delivered on "Plato and Modern Education," by an Oxford classicist, Sir Richard Livingstone. This age, he argues, needs as no other age has needed "a sense of values by which to judge and use the gifts of material civilization." Plato's "concern was to impart values." Yet, "as for sermonizing, a sense of values is perhaps best imparted by those who feel them intensely but never mention them." We cannot improve on Plato's idea: "When the child goes to school, 'the works of great poets are put into his hands, and he learns them by heart,' that he may see what human greatness is and desire to imitate it."

Quotations from Homer and Horace no longer flavor debates in Parliament, but the classics are emphatically taught in the secondary and in the public schools, and all students who enter the great universities have passed examinations in the classics. The classics are going on in the direction of total eclipse, but they are not likely to be booted out any time soon in order to make way for a smattering of Spanish useful for automobile salesmen in South America. Reforms, no matter how drastic, are not likely to trade off the whole classical tradition for a Dismal Swamp of "Education" courses designed by their "unctuous elaboration of the obvious" to stultify any mind subjected to them — courses politically useful, however, to the professors who give them, for thus they are kept in jobs, and politically useful also to the students who take them because the Education monopolists have manipulated laws to bar even the humblest job in most American public schools to any applicant who has not spent his or her golden youth in massing Education credits. . . . But I was talking about science.

The English school system certainly needs to be made more democratic. The Industrial Revolution began in England. Development of it there, however, has not brought anything like the sanitation, comforts and conveniences to the masses that development has brought in America. Some Americans have had much to say for the "natural pattern" of life in contrast to the pattern of machines. Witness in one sector alone the contemporary books and pictures idealizing the Pueblo Indian "way of life." Yet if you are going to be machined, the solution would seem to lie in having the very best of machinery. England is as machined as America, but not so efficiently machined. I have no idea which set of machine drivers is happier. I myself have been happier in an old rattletrap of a truck than in the highest-powered de luxe car. Happiness is not machine-tooled. It seems to me that English conservatism has, even in the midst of machines, held on to pre-machine humanism in such a way that English life is distinctly less metallic than American.

The American tends to regard the world as physical and, therefore, to consider everything in it as improvable by means of a new model. No other Christian people have conceived God as being so nearly the spit and image of themselves. The Rotarians like a preacher who pictures Christ for them as a Rotarian.

The elements of materialism and of idealism may be of about equal weight in Uncle Sam and John Bull. They are not blended in each according to the same chemical formula. Tennyson's Northern Farmer, who always heard the hoof-beats of his horse saying "Proputty, proputty, proputty," would hardly have sold the hawthorn hedges off his land for any other kind of property. An American agriculturist visiting in England recently advised against hedges as taking up too much soil space; barbed wire fences would take up less space and serve just as well to separate fields. He seemed to overlook the material fact that hedges afford protection for animals and for tender plants against harsh winds. He took into no account how hedges shelter and feed the wonderful bird life of England and how the more birds there are in the hedges, the fewer bugs in the garden. He left out the country's deep-seated and for centuries established appreciation of the charm, the graciousness and the loveliness that hedges give the landscape.

In the best newspapers of England and Scotland, readers contribute letters that thrash out opinions, principles, politics, and call upon history. I don't know whether the editors or the contributors are responsible for such a small percentage of the letters confining themselves to private bellyaches and ignorant eulogies of base politicians, along with ignorant denouncements of anything not moving to the immediate financial advancement of the writer. I have read one of these letters calling upon the present generation to "acknowledge its indebtedness to the past and then, once and for all, to shut the door upon it." I cannot conceive, however, of the British as erecting into a national hero a Henry Ford with his motto, "History is bunk."

The British, in the words of Mr. Winston Churchill, have peculiarly "reconciled democracy and tradition," in an "interplay and interweaving of past and present," making for "the historical continuity of our island life." The discovery of the wheel was more important and revolutionary to the human race than the development of Ford's tin Lizzie. Though the wheel had been in use thousands of years before Columbus sailed, no wheel up to that time had lightened a burden or accelerated motion on the American continents; nor had their inhabitants ever used a sail to harness the wind's power. The man for whom history is bunk is almost invariably as obtuse to the future as he is blind to the past. Henry Ford's feudalistic opposition to labor unions is an example in proof of the statement.

To be conscious of "historical continuity" is to be tempered with conservatism. If this conservatism regards the spiritual values of the past and not its mere outworn shells, it stands as a guarantee for spiritual values in the future. It would be a sad thing if no voice regretted the threat by factory towers and coal smoke to the splendor that has so long fallen upon the castle walls of Durham and to the wild pristine loveliness of Loch Lomond. Hunger for the beauty that the past has created assures us that, somehow, the future will cherish and create it. The loss of a beautiful creation of antiquity, whether that loss comes from barbaric destruction or from the necessities of a newly ordered society, is nothing compared to the loss in human beings of a yearning for what is noble and beautiful.

"I love everything that's old: old friends, old times, old manners, old books, old wine." And this kind of Oliver Goldsmith heart conserving what has been is as far removed from reactionary greed as humanity is from flint.

3

August 3, 1944. I have spent an hour reading the speech that it took the Prime Minister one hundred minutes to deliver in the House of Commons yesterday. Some of its passages I reread. In these days of pilotless bombs when Pale Death with impartial foot knocks at the doors of poor men's hovels and of kings' palaces, droning, hovering, diving over every magazine of stores by the vast docks and every little shop along the thousands of miles of London streets, the house where Parliament sits may not be described. But all the drama of human causes, and of names become household familiarities down the sweep of centuries, that Macaulay attached to the Hall of William Rufus as it witnessed the impeachment of Warren Hastings lived in that unnamed building where Churchill spoke yesterday.

The current of liberalism, concreted in Beveridge plans for common men, has been running against Churchill in this country; while the counter-current, the current of reactionaryism, has been running against Roosevelt in America. The private talk I have heard against Churchill seems to come more from sorrow than from anger. After the war is over, the opposition will strengthen. It is, of course, not as a conservative that the name of Winston Churchill will live as long as the English language is on the records; it is as a great spiritual voice as well as a material force, never deviating or flagging, in a war against the powers of evil. Mr. Churchill is a reactionary with a vast difference.

Reaction in America since the Civil War has had in its hard lust for profits and corporation expansion almost nothing of spiritual regret for the light of other days. A domed Teapot smoldering with crude oil might be taken as its symbol. Any human structure that rises to nobility is infused with spirit. The fires of nobility, burning slow and unquenchably like caldrons of lava deep in the earth's center, light up every speech that Churchill of the Wars has ever made for the guidance of the people whose genius he supremely represents.

"There is a notable difference," he said yesterday, between ideology and idealism. "While I cherish idealism as a cheerful light playing over the hopes of men and inspiring noble deeds, ideology too often presents itself as undue regimentation of ideas and may very likely be incompatible with freedom. . . .

"For forty years I have been a consistent friend of France and its brave army. All my life I have been grateful for the contribution France has made to the culture, glory and, above all, the sense of personal liberty and the rights of man which have radiated from the soul of France. . . .

"I never liked Trotsky, but there is one thing he said at the time of the brutal German treaty of Brest-Litovsk which stuck in my mind. He said to the German bullies: 'The destiny of a great nation has never yet been settled by the temporary condition of its technical apparatus.' "

Mr. Churchill did not become the King's first minister "in order to preside over the liquidation of the British Empire." In this harsh world, the good as well as the evil policies of nations depend on power. Earthly power is materialistic, and the powerful are and always will be ready to maintain the *status quo*. Mr. Churchill is the very epitome of John Bull conservatism inherent in power, but he also epitomizes that human nobility which, justifying the power — and the conservatism — is always breaking out in English expression. In a speech in the House of Commons on the British Empire — and nobody has accused him of being a mouther of cant — he said: "I do not object [to considering] 'enlightened self-interest' [as one of] the various forces that hold the British Empire together. That has a valued and important part to play, but the honorable friend who used that expression would not, I am sure, make the mistake of placing 'enlightened self-interest' in front of those deeper and more mysterious influences which cause human beings to do most incalculable, improvident, and, from the narrow point of view, profitless things. It is our union in freedom, and for the sake of our way of living, which is the great fact, reinforced by tradition and sentiment, and it does not depend upon anything that could ever be written down in any account kept in some large volume."

The tears inherent in human affairs seldom drop from corporation eyes down into the pits where blackened men cog into machinery that grinds both them and coal into golden dust. The Churchillian conservatism may not be directed towards equalitarianism, but it does not leave one empty, baffled, as does that conservatism standing only for the prosperity of spiritless property. It is always infused with a sympathy for human kind. Many times I have thought back to that twenty-second day of June in 1941

when Hitler invaded Russia and when tens of millions of
English-speaking people dispersed over the globe listened
to Churchill's voice. "Here this summer evening," he said,
"I see the Russian soldiers standing on the threshold of
their native land, guarding the fields which their fathers
have tilled from time immemorial. I see them guarding
their homes where mothers and wives pray — ah, yes, for
there are times when all pray — for the safety of their loved
ones, the return of the bread-winner, of their champion,
of their protector. I see the ten thousand villages of Russia, where the means of existence were wrung so hardly
from the soil, but where there are still primordial human
joys, where maidens laugh and children play." In those
words I seemed to hear the ringing of the Angelus for bent
peasants listening in their fields, as Millet's sad and beautiful colors have fixed them for the ages.

A man may react against a plan for society without violating "the temples of man's freedom and man's honor" and
without denying the dignity of life — though many reactionaries prating about idealism do both. When at last in
1939 Britain rose to fight for the civilization of freedom
against the barbarism of dictators, Prime Minister Neville
Chamberlain said, "It is a sad day for us all." Taking up
the word, Winston Churchill said: "Indeed it is a sad day,"
but in making war "to establish on impregnable rocks the
rights of the individual," and "to establish and revive the
stature of man," the nation may be "conscious of another
note." The "sad" days for him really lay back in the years
when he had to drink from the bitter cup brewed not
alone by Nazi brutes but also by the lepers of moral apathy

and immoral triviality whitening the nations that confessed allegiance to decency and liberty. His own nature could feel nothing but release now that the long dormant forces to which he, never dormant, belonged had roused themselves to fight against what all good men know to be Evil. Even if the fight ended in national poverty and personal death, there were worse things than either.

I do not apprehend the isolationist argument against allying with other English-speaking nations, as well as with nations that do not speak English, on the grounds that Great Britain has no intention of "liquidating" the empire. If it be admitted that the British are a decent people, then their conservatism, however exasperating, awkward and stupid its manifestations may at times appear, guarantees the reliability and durability so desired by every contracting party in another. When the South Americans swear by *la palabra Inglés* — the word of an Englishman — they are paying tribute to this conservatism. It has the character that, in the phrase of the West, "will do to ride the river with." After partners have picked each other on the solid grounds that each will do to ride the river with, they do not proceed to try to suck the lifeblood out of each other. Good partners trust each other, rejoice in the prosperity of each other. They are not out to do each other. Their just co-operation will benefit their neighbors as well as themselves.

CHAPTER VII
Rememberers

NOT ALL conservative people remember, but all people who remember with love must be profoundly conservative in some ways. Their memories themselves are a conservation of what has been.

> And I swear as I thought of her thus in that hour,
> And how after all old things are best,
> I smelt the smell of that jasmine flower
> That she used to wear in her breast.

One cannot conceive of any possessor of what we call a soul as being without remembrance of things past.

I

People talk and write about the soul of France and the spirit of Paris as easily as they sing about the sidewalks of New York. It is seldom suggested that London has a soul. People who know that their feet are on the ground are shy of mentioning souls. When a man does not know anything in particular about a city or a nation, he can babble about its soul. I have no intention of writing about London; I still feel that I am going east to Westminster Bridge over the Thames when I know I am going west. Yet something individual in the pulse of London life is as detectable anywhere in this vast city as the soul of Chicago is undetectable.

I was going into the Reform Club with a Londoner whose years are marked by tolerance and understanding, when he said, "The reason I had rather be in London than any other place in the world is that nothing can happen anywhere else without its happening also in London." This was going beyond Disraeli's saying that "London is a nation, not a city." It was a variation of Emerson's saying that "London is the epitome of our times." Since Emerson's day New York has become far richer than London and the Bank of England must sometimes sign on the dotted line indicated by the Federal Reserve Bank, but London remains "the clearinghouse of the world." America has become more powerful than the British Empire, but somehow the center of the world's gravity is still London. The "marshaling of affairs" at any nucleus of population anywhere on earth radiates to London. No country, of course, can be isolated; London has never imagined that she was isolated. Nothing can happen elsewhere without its happening also in London, not because London is the supreme world compeller, but because London is the supreme world receiver. The cowboy of the lone prairie was buried in London also. John Wesley's house is in London; so are houses built for the Italian cardinals. "When a man is tired of London," Doctor Johnson declared, "he is tired of life; for there is in London all that life can afford." Doctor Johnson was a Londoner. If the world wars have depleted

Britain — and they have — they have made London afford
even more than Doctor Johnson found in it. Yet it does
not impose itself on the island, does not swallow up the
expressers of national thought as New York so often does
for America.

The place where the London tides of humanity flow
strongest for me is Trafalgar Square, at Charing Cross. I
have gone there again and again to sense those tides, as a
person will walk daily to some point on the seashore to hear
and see and feel the everlasting surf. The Square is an
island around which millions of people and thousands of
buses and other motor cars pass, on their way to and from
somewhere, daily. On the island thousands, many seeming
to have no other destination, loiter, ebb in and ebb out,
among them always children feeding the pigeons, always
lovers, always old men and old women who would feel
the day lost and abnormal unless they came to Trafalgar
Square, always soldiers and seamen from the four quarters
of the globe seeing Trafalgar Square eagerly for the first
time, always a bobby or two seeming to see nothing, yet
seeing all.

I went there the first time for the specific purpose of
saluting the figure of Admiral Nelson on top of the lofty
column, guarded by Landseer's four massive lions — Nelson not only of Trafalgar, but of Britain's ocean tradition.
There were perhaps two hundred pigeons flocking down
on a small space of the raised expanse of the Square. They
were concentrating on some crumbs an old woman was
scattering sparingly. A playful dog kept dashing into their
midst, at which the pigeons would fly up, wheel and settle

uneasily back, much to the dog's joy and that of us idlers. I rather wondered that a policeman did not remonstrate with the dog or with the dog's unrevealed owner. Perhaps the policeman figured that if the pigeons had the freedom of the air the dog was due that of the ground. Anyhow, the policeman had his eye on another free creature, which the dog may have been jealous of, for few people enjoy more than a dog being the central attraction.

The Nelson column rests on a ponderous base raised three feet or so above the pavement where the dog sported with the pigeons. Here on this elevation his opponent for attention posed in a posture as immobile as Nelson's bronze. The figure was a tall, gaunt man, draped in a long overcoat, in the attitude of a praying Moslem, kneeling with forearms and hands on the ground, face between hands. How long he had been thus fixed on the pedestal when I saw him, I do not know, nor how he had climbed up there. His enduring stillness seemed to arouse the policeman's curiosity. The policeman walked over to the pedestal, getting as near the kneeling figure as he could, and stood a long time facing him, saying nothing. I have heard old trail drivers tell about horses freezing to death in a blizzard standing up, cold death coming to them so equably that the center of gravity in the bodies was not disturbed. I knew the praying man had not frozen to death; the weather was mild and the sun was shining. The policeman got tired of watching the figure, would not disturb his salaam or interfere with his liberty to be odd, and walked back. Still the kneeler kneeled in immobility. The pigeons had grown tired of affording fun to the dog and flown away. I wondered what the kneeler would do if the dog, lifted by somebody on to the pedestal, should begin sniffing at his heels.

Then the prostrate figure arose with a bound, leaped off the pedestal, and rushed across the square. He had a rusty beard, did not look like a prophet. I walked over to the policeman with a query. "He's touched in the head," the policeman said. "He comes here often. He kneels at the Soldiers' Cenotaph in Whitehall, by the Unknown Soldier in Westminster Abbey, in other public places. . . . No, I don't know what he is praying for."

I can remember when I read Southey's life of Nelson; I can't remember when Nelson's name was not heroic to me. The English sea dogs and the Confederate soldiers have always been my ideal fighters. I'm thinking of something beyond bravery or efficiency. The R.A.F. when Britain stood alone in this war had everything. After the fight of the *Revenge* against the fifty-three Spanish ships in the Azores —

God of battles, was ever a battle like this in the world before? —

its captain, wounded to death,

     . . . rose upon their decks, and he cried:
"I have fought for Queen and Faith like a valiant man and
   true;
I have only done my duty as a man is bound to do:
With a joyful spirit I Sir Richard Grenville die!"
And he fell upon their decks, and he died.

It would be hard to say what one man of the past comes nearest to being the national hero of England. It might be

Shakespeare. In the realms of action, Nelson certainly
leads.

> They lie beyond the reach of human pride
> Who fought with Nelson and with Nelson died.

The imperial hand that surrendered its sword at Waterloo
had long back been paralyzed by Nelson and the British
fleet. Considering how this fleet was for nearly a hundred
years to enforce the Monroe Doctrine, Nelson might well
be one of America's heroes also.

His ghost appeared to me by the monument, not noble,
at Great Yarmouth while I looked out over the North Sea
and remembered a phrase out of World War I's bravest
ballad, "The Admiral's Ghost," by Alfred Noyes.

> Do'ee know who Nelson was?
> That poor little shrivelled form,
> With the patch on his eye and the pinned-up sleeve
> And a soul like a North Sea storm? . . .
>
> Nelson — was Francis Drake!
> Oh, what matters the uniform,
> Or the patch on your eye or your pinned-up sleeve,
> If your soul's like a North Sea storm?

And now, thanks to that fine gentleman, Admiral Sir
Charles Little, I stood in Portsmouth harbor aboard the
Victory, on which Nelson sent up his immortal message,
won his greatest victory, and died. A brass plate on the
quarterdeck says, "HERE NELSON FELL." Below, in the dim
light of hanging lanterns — how dim it must have seemed to
the surgeons! — you see where he died, October 12, 1805 —

ten years before Waterloo. The two longest-headed institutions in the world are the British nation and the Roman
Catholic Church.

Nelson had spent the better part of his forty-seven
years at sea. At Cape St. Vincent in 1797 he defeated the
Spanish fleet; in Aboukir Bay, in Egypt, in 1798, a French
fleet; at Copenhagen, in 1801, the Danish fleet. His idea was
to annihilate Napoleon's sea power. He had chased the
main French fleet for over two years when he finally engaged it off Cape Trafalgar. He was a little man with a
weak body; he had lost an arm and an eye in battles. It
was about noon on that October day when he signaled,
"England expects every man to do his duty." His ship
grappled with the French *Redoubtable*. He insisted on
coming down onto the quarterdeck so that he could see.
Big Captain Hardy was with him when a French musket
ball went through his lungs and spine, lodging in the
muscles of his back. Hardy tried to raise him.

"They've done for me at last, Hardy," he said.

"I hope not."

"Yes, my backbone is shot through."

He lived for three hours, mostly conscious, after they
carried him below. Hardy brought him word that fourteen or fifteen enemy ships had surrendered.

"That's well," he said. "I bargained for twenty." It was
twenty before he died.

He said, "Remember, I leave Lady Hamilton and my
daughter Horatia as a legacy to my country."

Again, "Kiss me, Hardy."

Then, "Thank God. I have done my duty."

They brought his body back to England in alcohol and buried it in Saint Paul's Cathedral, which still stands, though the Germans bombed it and bombed acres of buildings around it out of existence. A seaman who guided me over the *Victory* volunteered that sailors could hardly have drunk the alcohol in which Nelson's body was pickled, as the old story has it, since the container was placed in Nelson's cabin forward, where no seaman ever went except on a special duty.

I noticed that the flag on the *Victory* was at half mast and asked why. The seaman said, "They're flying it at half mast for two months out of respect for the death of your First Lord of the Admiralty."

I did not think it necessary to tell him that Colonel Knox's official title was Secretary of the Navy.

And so, for me, the people and the pigeons on Trafalgar Square are tempered by "a soul like a North Sea storm." It does not make any difference which way I walk from Trafalgar Square. The names of the streets are like old songs, because of their familiarity out of the world's greatest literature. Just the names make an unending poem, full of connotations: Leadenhall, Threadneedle and Lombard, where the banks are; Cheapside, Ludgate Hill and Paternoster Row, where the Germans burned up millions of books; Fleet Street of the journalists; Chancery Lane of the courts; the Strand to walk upon; Pall Mall, Haymarket, Piccadilly Circus, rich Regent Street; Bond, of the fashions; Whitehall, of power; Jermyn, where the barrel organ plays; Berkeley Square, where Tomlinson "gave up his ghost."

2

It is good to remember. On Memorial Day I went out for the first time to the American Cemetery not far from Cambridge. I have been back since several times. Thrice weekly taps blow over new graves and then the faraway bugle responds, making the finest earthly sound that a soldier being put back to earth could have. This cemetery is on a gentle hill-slope, looking far away to the east and to the north. On two sides of it are tall woods famous for nightingale singing in the spring. On the other two sides are fields that skylarks soar and sing over through spring and summer and on into fall. The sky above is a vast pathway for war planes, and as I have known this spot only in wartime, they seem to me as much in place as the great flocks of rooks that stream from far places at evening to roost in the trees of Madingley woods.

The land was a field tilled by a farmer who loved this plot of soil and was skilled in working it. Rows of graves and the avenues between them harmonize with the lovely hillside and the woods and the soft faraway prospect. The ground will always be beautifully kept. I have never been there without seeing fresh flowers at some of the markers and wreaths from civilians as well as from military organizations on the pedestal above which the Stars and Stripes fly at half mast. American airmen are making the beautiful old church in Madingley village under the hill a memorial chapel. In ranks silent and orderly, row by row, recruited thrice a week, their comrades lie in a place fitting for the long peace.

The great American public tends to remember by special days. The English seem to remember with a difference. The constant flowers on graves in country churchyards and on monuments to the war dead indicate an abiding remembrance; yet it is not the kind of remembrance that the Irish cherish, so harking back to wrongs under Cromwell that they cannot go forward three centuries afterward. "To quarrel with the past is to lose the future." There is no use crying over spilt milk. It is a steadying remembrance, as expressed in the prayer "Lest we forget." The gods are known by their long memories.

Daily *The Times* prints under "In Memoriam" a column of notices inserted and paid for by the rememberers. Not all of the notices concern the war dead; not all of the war dead are of this war. Here, "in proud beloved memory," is the name of one killed in the Jutland Battle, 1916. The manner in which people express "love's last gift," remembrance, is an index to the amplitude, or the smallness, of their natures. Anybody who reads through the "In Memoriam" column any day will be struck not only with the poignancy of human grief but with its ennoblement, memory encompassing causes and country and mankind itself. For instance: —

"In proud memory of my fine brother who in the fight for a better world gave his short life in operations over Germany.

All you had hoped for, all you had, you gave
To save mankind — yourselves you scorned to save."

Unwittingly, the rememberers reveal elements in that mixture that has made England not only powerful but great. "To our gay, beautiful only son. . . . He loved birds, and green places, and the wind on the heath, and he saw the brightness of the skirts of God." A father remembering a son killed in Libya quotes: —

> Horses he loved, laughter and the sun,
> A song, wide spaces, and the open air.
> The trust of all dumb living things he won,
> And never knew the luck too good to share.

On September 6 (1944) one who signed only his initials inserted this call to memory: —

"*The Marne.* — In honour of the first great victory in the World Wars still being waged. And to the glorious memory of those who, after a fighting retreat against an overwhelming enemy, turned, and were the first to cross the Marne.

> O little mighty Force your way is ours,
> This land inviolate your monument."

People get what they admire and dwell on. Go out tonight after supper and to a star repeat the old rhyme: —

Star, star, star bright, first star I see tonight,
I wish I may, I wish I might, have this wish I wish tonight.

If you wish to be a Hollywood star, you'll be Hollywoodish — if you keep on yearning that way. If you wish a million dollars, you'll get at least a dime, if you keep on really wanting dollars and cutting out everything else in order to get them. If you wish to be as eloquent as Churchill, you'll be eloquent to the extent of your capacity — provided that is your dominating aim. The wishing cap and the magic carpet of the fairy tales are only exaggerations of reality. To know what people admire is to know what they themselves are.

The poor and humble do not get represented much in *The Times*. Some of them have feelings about the exclusiveness of the officers' ranks in the British Army, though the last war and this one have done much to destroy that exclusiveness. It is claimed that the "tight little governing club" even while expressing its own unquestioned patriotism admits only in a patronizing way the nobility of the patriotism of the masses. However all this may be, and it is not my theme, I do think that the voluntary characterizations of "Fallen Officers," Americans often among them, published daily by *The Times*, alongside lists of the British forces killed or missing in action, represent what the country as a whole admires in leadership.

Major J. R. D. "Had he lived, he would undoubtedly have played full part in the reforms and changes our educational system may undergo, for while a keen supporter of the public schools, he was eager that their benefits should be more widely spread."

Lieutenant R. W. "His temperament was fiery. Injustice enraged him as much as ugliness. The developments of modern persecution and such actions as the Italian attack on Ethiopia moved him deeply. His sense of outraged humanity prepared him in the years before the war for what was coming, and caused him, when it came, to give up his career as an artist and welcome that of a soldier."

Brigadier-General Theodore Roosevelt. "Invalided to London, it was hard to hold him down, as he longed to be with his troops training for the invasion of France. He was warned that men of 56 must be careful after pneumonia. Yet if you know the breed, you will know that you might as well warn the wind not to blow. So his stout heart failed and he has died, as he would have chosen, in a tent on the field of battle, with memories of a brave life left behind him and honors thick upon him."

Captain W. R. B. H. "He spent many of his evenings as a poor man's lawyer in North London, where he earned the gratitude of many to whom he was able to bring advice and comfort."

Lieutenant R. G. W. "Particular parts of England meant much to him. Had he been told that the price of their preservation would be his life, he would have laughed and said that it was probably worth it."

Captain J. W. B. "Tall, lean and jaunty, Joe had inherited a full measure of the charm of his maternal grandfather, Cyril Maude (the actor). He persuaded Oxford contemporaries to spend nights with him at Borley Rectory, 'the most haunted house in England,' and with their aid made a series of observations for the Society of Psychical Research. Confident that the war in Europe would soon be over, he was already planning what he might do in the Pacific war, preferably in China."

Colonel F. P. M. "Mackie made many contributions to medical literature. Perhaps his most important and original work was on the part played by the louse in the transmission of relapsing fever; but it was in the administrative sphere of tropical hygiene that his gifts were most widely appreciated. His activities ranged over Tibet, India, Burma, Iraq, and tropical Africa, and he advanced the knowledge of such diseases as plague, kala azar, malaria, spirillum fever, sleeping sickness, and other tse-tse fly diseases. Neither fads nor fancies nor self-interest obscured his professional or social affairs. He was a good speaker, lucid, balanced, and brief. He was always gay and ready of wit, especially in difficulties. His life is a record of good work and good fellowship."

Major D. de S. B. "As a small boy he performed in A. A. Milne's *The Red Feathers*. He combined in an extraordinary degree the qualities of a man of action with the sensitiveness of the dreamer. He hated the destruction that war entails; yet he confessed himself 'in love with the action it brings.' In one of his last letters home, he said, 'I have a rose in my buttonhole, very unmilitary, but good for one's sanity.' Metaphorically, he always did wear a rose in his buttonhole. It is to be hoped that some of his poems will be collected and his painting exhibited."

Lieutenant R. G. A. "Killed on a torpedoed destroyer. He could be impish and annoy the solemn, and he loved the out-of-the-way and could make other people see the value of it. He knew about the truth of things and was happy, lovable and strong."

Major M. H. "He had that serenity which comes only from true peace of mind. He was loved by the country people in Norfolk and by the natives of Uganda. His courtesy was not artificial or merely the fruit of good breeding; it sprang from a deep reverence towards humanity."

Lieutenant E. F. "He derived from his lovely home at Bowood his early developed appreciation in scenery and art. Where he was, there the world always seemed an amusing and original kind of place. His comical mimicry showed insight into character. He would have gone far in the parliamentary service of his country on which he had set his heart."

I have picked out passages emphasizing those qualities of mind and spirit that go to make a civilization. The emphasis is on being, not on possessing; on duty, not on rights and privileges; on sensitiveness to the beautiful and on cultivated intelligence, not on getting ahead; on rounded natures, in which spirited wit plays. Morals are taken for granted. Nothing that is said would be foreign to American readers. Yet the cumulative emphasis affords a far better index to something English and British than the everlasting contrasts between beer at natural temperature in Britain and beer ice-cold in America, between "lorry" and "truck," driving to the left instead of to the right, keeping a railroad ticket for a collector at the end of a journey instead of giving it to a conductor on the train, and many other divergencies as inconsequential as the difference between Tweedledee and Tweedledum.

3

Centuries ago a landholder in the vicinity of Bury St. Edmunds became lost in the darkness. His concern for other people who might suffer in the same way prompted him to erect a bell tower and to ring its bell in the gathering darkness every evening. When he died, he left the rent from a close of land to keep the bell ringing. This kind of civilized concern for society, the concern of the aged man who plants an acorn that it may grow into a tree of graciousness for distant generations, is not confined to any century or notion. It has been more common since Benjamin Franklin's time than during any preceding age, however, and it is more prevalent in Great Britain than in any other country.

The list of wills and bequests published daily by *The Times* necessarily limits itself to the more important properties. An astonishing percentage of the bequeathers leave something for public benefactions. I have read that there are about 10,000 organizations for the public good in the country. Many organizations advertise modestly, merely suggesting immediate or testamentary aid. They seem to go on the assumption that calling their existence to the attention of the just-minded with property is sufficient. They do not shout their needs and their virtues. Their style of appeal must pay with the British or they would not keep on advertising. For instance, out of the "Personal" column I clip this five-line advertisement, next to one offering a used portable typewriter for one hundred and five dollars: —

"All Ranks and All Services. — On widespread battle-fronts are men and women whose time of greatest need will be in the years to come — AFTER service. You can help now by a legacy to EARL HAIG'S BRITISH LEGION APPEAL FUND, Cardigan House, Richmond, Surrey."

Some of the wills and bequests may be interesting. The first figure in each example represents the net value of the estate (aside from land). A pound equals four dollars.

"£5,116. He left residue, after a life interest, equally between the World's Evangelization Mission, the Church Army, the China Inland Mission, Dr. Barnardo's Homes, and the Friends' Caravan Mission."

"£8,729. She left residue to the Treasury 'to help to pay for the cost of the present war.' "

"£21,038. She left £1,000 to the International Holiness Mission, for erecting a church in South Africa."

"£542,845. He left £1,000 each to the R.A.F. Benevolent Fund and the Cancer Hospital."

"£23,895. She left £1,000 to the Dr. Gordon Roberts Hospital, India; £1,000 to Aberystwyth and Cardiganshire General Hospital; £500 each to the Welsh Presbyterian Church of Wales Foreign Mission, Tower Hamlets Mission, London Temperance Hospital, Hospital for Incurables, Streatham, and the Slum Child Welfare and Social Service of the South London Mission; and residue between Dr. Gordon Roberts Hospital, Foreign Mission of the Welsh Presbyterian Church of Wales, Hospital for Incurables, Tower Hamlets Mission, and National Institute for the Blind."

"Thirty-four hospitals and other charitable institutions will benefit under the will leaving £486,755."

"£19,038. He left the buildings and land known as the Bunbury Men's Club to the Bunbury branch of the British Legion, and £500 to the fabric fund of Bunbury Church."

"£10,701. She left a residue to the Waifs and Strays Society; Cancer Hospital, Fulham; St. Dunstan's; Star and Garter Homes for Sailors and Soldiers; and Roehampton Military Hospital."

"£323,344. He left £10,000 to Edinburgh University to be applied within 12 months for the purpose of founding a chair of lectureship in Orthopaedics."

"£11,321. She left the greater part of her property to the Milner General Hospital, Greenwich."

"£358,923. She left a sum sufficient for the purchase of land and the erection of cottage homes for six widows of seamen, with weekly allowances of ten shillings and provision of lighting and fuel; and one half of residue to Queen Anne's Bounty and one-half to the Royal Masonic Benevolent Institution."

" £5,093. He left residue to Woolwich and Plumstead War Memorial Hospital."

" £34,188. She left £500 to the Society for the Propagation of the Gospel in Foreign Parts; £100 to the Princess Elizabeth Orthopaedic Hospital; and the residue between the Royal United Kingdom Beneficent Association, the National Benevolent Association, the Governesses' Benevolent Institute, and the Working Ladies' Guild."

" £12,310. She left the proceeds of the sale of her freehold residence to the Society for the Protection of Animals in North Africa."

" £12,070. She left £1,000 to St. Joseph's Nursing Home; £500 to the Converts' Aid Society; and £500 to Hilda Bourne, for use in her work at the Catholic Settlement."

" £2,506. She left her freehold residence, College View, to the R.N.L.I.; the proceeds from the sale of her furniture, etc. to the Salvation Army; and £700 Defence Bonds to the Mission to Seamen, Hull."

" £357,091. He left, subject to a life interest, £15,000 to the University of Manchester; £5,000 to the Victoria University of Manchester; and £500 to Manchester Ear Hospital."

" £28,081. She left residue equally between the British Empire Cancer Campaign and the Sisterhood of the Holy Rood, Findon."

" £310,798. He left £1,000 to the Worshipful Company of Stationers and Newspaper Makers, and parts of the residue to the Printers' Pension Fund and National Advertising Benevolent Society and to King Edward VII Hospital Fund (with the request that they pay £5,000 to Worthing Hospital)."

In countries of capitalistic civilization the vast accumulations of wealth into the hands of organizations classed, for taxable purposes, as "benevolent," always tends to unbalance the economy. To restore the balance, the state may, from century to century, have to expropriate the properties, as has been done over and over with church estates,

Lest one good custom should corrupt the world.

The implications concerning society are large and far-reaching in the recently published wills of two owners of landed estates. Sir Richard Ackland, a member of Parliament, in turning over his Devon and Somerset estates to the National Trust, was reported thus: —

"Holding his political views, he said, the ownership of such an extensive property had been an increasingly heavy burden on his conscience. It was more important that the estate should continue as a well-run agricultural community than that it should be owned by him or one of his successors.

"Death Duties [inheritance taxes] would have compelled the sale of a portion of the property on his death, and the remainder would have to be broken up when his son died. This would mean that farms would be sold over the heads of tenants and desirable building sites sold to builders. If he had continued to own these estates for his own life, then in two generations both the estates would have ceased to exist. Now they were safe for ever.

"He was glad to know that the income that was his would now be available primarily for the improvement of the estate, and that the property was secure forever from the sort of disintegration which had overtaken similar estates in other parts of the country."

On the other hand, Sir Francis Edward Fremantle, of Hertfordshire, in bequeathing the estate of Bedwell Park to his son, published a contrary conception of duty to society. His will declares: —

Whereas by the goodness of Almighty God I have been entrusted with the use and disposal of the estates earned by the industry and enterprise of my dear mother's forefathers,

And whereas it appears to have been the wish of my grandfather, the late Sir Culling Eardley, that they should be held as a whole for the use of his descendants and the maintenance of a family centre,

And whereas England depends for the welfare of all sections and for her share in the world's work in no small degree on the wise and sympathetic co-operation in her country life of a resident landed gentry,

I do hereby devise these Estates to others in confidence that they will so use and enjoy their rights and fulfil their duties as to carry out the general intentions of those by whom they have been bequeathed.

It is my hope, without making any trust, that future owners of the estate, so long as the above intentions can best be so served, and without prejudicing the claim of the public interest for enterprise, leadership or useful service elsewhere, will live at Bedwell in simple manner, be hospitable, generous and helpful to friends and neighbours, will service God, the King and their fellow citizens to the utmost of their power and opportunity, and will devote their lives and the possessions entrusted to them to the good of the whole community in Church and State.

4

Sifted to the bottom, the burden of all these wills and bequests is to remember obligations. I always look for those monuments and inscriptions memorializing the past that say, as it were, "In this sign shalt thou conquer." In cathedrals I enjoy most the arches and ceilings, actually very heavy, but seeming through architectural skill to rise like gossamer towards heaven. It was not this lifting up at the Norwich Cathedral, however, that gave me an unforgettable impression. It was a very simple grave outside, and the very simple inscription on it. The grave is back of the cathedral, close to the wall, near trees, in a place of great peace. During the past two years thousands of American soldiers have paused and read the inscription on the small wooden plaque at the foot of the grave — or passed by unreading. The inscription says: —

TO THE PURE AND HOLY MEMORY OF EDITH CAVELL, WHO GAVE HER LIFE FOR ENGLAND, OCT. 12, 1915. HER NAME LIVETH FOR-EVER.

Born in 1865 at Swardeston, Norfolk, where her father was Vicar 46 years, she became matron of a Red Cross hospital in Brussels in 1914, where she tended English, French, Belgian and German soldiers with equal care. She helped in escape of her countrymen and of those allied to them and after some months of success she was arrested by the German authorities in Brussels and sentenced to death. After ten weeks' imprisonment she was executed early in the morning of October 12th, 1915. Her last words conclude with what some have considered the greatest utterance of the War. Here are her actual words: —

"I HAVE NO FEAR OF SHRINKING: I HAVE SEEN DEATH SO OFTEN THAT IT IS NOT STRANGE OR FEARFUL TO ME. I THANK GOD FOR THIS TEN-WEEKS QUIET BEFORE THE END. LIFE HAS ALWAYS BEEN HURRIED AND FULL OF DIFFICULTY. THIS TIME OF REST HAS BEEN A GREAT MERCY. THEY HAVE ALL BEEN VERY KIND TO ME HERE. BUT THIS I WOULD SAY, STANDING AS I DO IN VIEW OF GOD AND ETERNITY. I REALIZE THAT PATRIOTISM IS NOT ENOUGH. I MUST HAVE NO HATRED OR BITTERNESS TOWARDS ANYONE."

While I was standing before the plaque, copying down the words, three American soldiers came up. I moved to one side. They stood in silence and read. As they started to walk away, one said quietly, "So they killed her." Another one said, also quietly, "And look how we are treating that German woman who killed our men in France."

There was, of course, a sundial in the cathedral yard. All gardens and many walls in this land have sundials. Their plenitude where opportunities for marking the time are so restricted is but an indication of the love of the sun. One might imagine that a large society of Sun Worshipers had

mined the landscape with sundials to entice or trap the sun.
When the sun does shine, it is a joy to see the people in
parks and meadows and along lanes stretched out to get
it full length, little children butterflying in it, old people
bringing the chairs out of their houses to sit in it, lovers
pair by pair forgetting it. Yet it cannot be said as the old
Spanish sundial motto has it, *"No hay sabor sin sol."* (There
is no savor without the sun.) Sunshine or no sunshine, the
English fields are green and the flowers in season glad-
some. Looking at the sundials, I often recall William Haz-
litt's beautiful and melancholy essay on the subject. He
gives what must be the loveliest sundial motto in the world,
its original in Latin: I NUMBER ONLY THE HOURS THAT ARE
SERENE. The most fitting motto on a sundial I have seen in
England is at an old hall near Bedford: —

> FROM THE RISING OF THE SUN
> UNTIL THE GOING DOWN OF THE SAME
> THE LORD'S NAME IS TO
> BE PRAISED.

It is a fine thing for people to have noble words em-
blazoned where they can be commonly read. At Bedford,
John Bunyan was born; and in its jail he wrote at least a
part of *Pilgrim's Progress*, which, whether read nowadays
or not, is still one of the dozen great books of the world.
The sculptured figure of Bunyan looks out with vitality
over the public square at Bedford, and on its massive base are
these words: "IT HAD EYES LIFTED UP TO HEAVEN, THE BEST
OF BOOKS IN HIS HAND. THE LAW OF TRUTH WAS WRITTEN
UPON HIS LIPS. . . . IT STOOD AS IF IT PLEADED WITH MEN."

In the museum at Norwich I saw many of our soldiers, mostly lingering before the cases and stands of old battle gear and other artifacts, seldom pausing before a picture in the art galleries. One soldier in particular that I noticed did pause — to adjust his cap before the framed glass over a picture that shows a great tide going down from a stern and rock-bound coast, a bleak mountainside rising from the water without a sign of man on it. I could hear the water lapping and the wave breaking and the everlasting surf soughing. Underneath the picture are inscribed these words: —

> Mine ancient enemy, the Sea, hath but retired for a while
> And will return again, anon, with untold fury.

And the soldier seemed well pleased with the tilt of his cap and with himself, and passed out of view. He was the soldier who the night before, after I had made a talk at his base, asked: "Is there anything we Americans can learn from this country?"

I want to go back to Kensington Gardens, where a piping figure, a wise owl looking out from the folds of bronze, and squirrels, rabbits and mice playing about the base, makes me remember the Peter Pan that Maude Adams witched the world with. "Please believe in fairies," she would say. We all did. It is good to remember.

CHAPTER VIII
Farmers, Fens and Earthworms

A GOVERNMENT agriculturalist had the car and the gasoline. He took along a veterinary, the local historian of Lincoln and me. I had arrived in Lincoln the preceding afternoon to make a talk on the Ranching Industry of America. My reward was to be this excursion into Lincolnshire, to see the noted Lincolnshire Red Shorthorn Cattle, their breeding ground, and samples of the breeders. As we turned off a paved highway for Major Rippin's farm, I was delighted with a huge flock of golden plover, mixed with many gulls, feeding in a meadow against a brook. These plover, commonly called peewits, make good eating and used to be killed, but they are strictly protected now on account of the energetic way they go after wireworms, which grow into beetles very destructive of potatoes and other produce. Rubbing soot on seed potatoes as a protection against the wireworms is an old country practice no longer much used. But the wheeling and lighting of more than a thousand of the beautiful birds had no connection in my mind with either crops or worms.

I

Major Rippin's house, the long, low barns and sheds back of it, and the haystacks, all said, "Get down and come in." He led us into a snug room, with ceiling just low enough to be right, where a cheerful fire was burning in the fireplace. A retired army officer of the last war, he has for twenty years been dairying and raising prize milk cows of the Lincolnshire breed. His wife soon brought in freshly made hot coffee with cream, and mince pie. He himself brought in a brown quart bottle of whisky with a pitcher of milk to dilute it with. I had not had anything but tea for breakfast. The night before I had been a guest in a home — a home of easy hospitality and an artesian well of anecdotes — where they drink coffee after dinner but not for breakfast, and being as I was in Rome, I had drunk like a Roman. I took to Mrs. Rippin's coffee like a wet pup on a cold night taking to a warm, dry saddle-blanket.

Right away the Major began talking about the English climate. He said he asked an Australian what he thought about the English climate, and the Australian replied that he didn't know England had any climate, that as far as he could see England didn't have anything but weather. Major Rippin said that another stranger came to England to enjoy the summer but overslept himself one morning and missed it. At this, the government agriculturalist said that last year summer came on a Sunday. "Well," the Major went on, "the British didn't collect their empire because they were trying to conquer the world; they were just looking for another climate." Then he told the old story about a country squire who upon being introduced to the Persian ambassador in London said, "They tell me that in your country you worship the sun." "So would you if you ever saw him," the Persian replied.

Meantime I was drinking my second cup of hot coffee and looking at the pictures on the wall of a sheep-killing dog beside a dead sheep, hounds chasing a stag across a glen in Scotland, a cave man about to club a wolf over a stag the wolf had pulled down, and at a fox tail, an otter's foot and a beautifully mounted trout. The objects on the wall told me that the Major liked other things in the country besides his cows. While he talked on, I could have thought I was back home listening to some old rawhides bragging in reverse about how dry the drought was in 1916, how if the wind is not blowing this way in the Panhandle it's blowing the other way, how a norther comes so sudden that it freezes sweat, and how we have the world beat in general on everything that's worst.

Looking out the window, I remarked on the enormous molehills on the lawn. The Major said he could not get anybody to trap moles these days; the price used to be a penny a mole and a skillful trapper could keep a farm clear of them. The Major told how to snare snipe at the place where they are accustomed to stick their long bills into the earth, after worms. The agriculturalist said the way to trap the big partridges in snow is to stick a quart-sized whisky bottle, mouth first, into the snow full length, withdraw it, and put grain at the bottom of the hole. He said a partridge would come along, see the grain, reach for it, lose his balance, fall in the hole head first and stay there struggling until somebody lifted him out or the snow melted. The Major laughed and said a vinegar bottle would do as well as a whisky bottle for catching partridges. I told them the way to catch a coon in America is to put a crawfish, of which the coons are very fond, in a jug with a mouth just big enough to admit the coon's open hand. Mr. Coon comes along, smells the delicious crawfish, reaches in, closes his hand over the prize, but can't pull his fist through the mouth of the jug. He won't turn loose — and he'll just stay there trying to pull the crawfish out until he starves to death or until the trapper comes along and nabs him.

Talking about liking the way of life a man is used to, the Major told about a railroad man named George. When George's time came to retire on account of old age, he said he couldn't bear the thought of getting away from the rumble and whistling and bell-ringing of trains. He told the superintendent that he knew of a discarded railway coach that would make a fine home for him and his old woman, if the company would just place it on a bit of siding near a village and let him take possession. The superintendent was glad to do this, and George was mighty pleased. One cold rainy winter day a year or so later, a train on which the superintendent was riding stopped at the siding and the superintendent crawled out to have a word with old George. He found him squatted out in the weather, all hunkered up, smoking his pipe. "My gracious alive, George," the superintendent said, "why don't you get inside where it's comfortable to smoke?" George didn't say anything. He just got up and motioned the superintendent to follow him. He walked up to the dilapidated old coach, rubbed the mist off the glass window, and pointed to a sign with his finger. The sign read NO SMOKING.

After we got planted with Major Rippin in that snug room, it was mighty hard to get up. After we got out and went to looking at his fine cattle, it was harder to get away. In manner, humor, hospitality and the way of having "ample time," he would pass for an old-time rancher any day.

Like the majority of dairymen in this country, he has "dual purpose" cows — good for both milk and beef. His Lincolnshire Reds have been selectively bred for milk-giving powers, but they are superb beef cattle. We drove for half an hour, passing an ancient castle, and came to where the Bembridge brothers raise Lincolnshire Reds for beef purposes exclusively. The prize yearling bull for which they paid over four thousand dollars was a beautiful creature, as were cows that when fat would weigh up close to a ton. If I had had a private freight plane, I would have mortgaged my life insurance, bought a half-dozen yearlings, and flown them to Live Oak County with the intention of just sitting in the shade and watching them grow. As the old cowboy song goes, in irony, "cowpunching is only fun."

I wouldn't say it is all fun for the seventy-five thousand privates in the Women's Land Army who are feeding hogs, plowing, milking, cleaning stalls, spreading manure and doing other kinds of farm labor over England and Wales. The ones I saw looked cheerful and hale, though not at all horsey. Their supervisor in the Lincoln area, who used to be a lady of leisure and grow great gardens of flowers, told me of a milliner from London's most fashionable district who took so to the work that after she had been on a farm for six months she was running it, six other women of the Land Army working under her. She refused to marry a Canadian colonel; all she wanted was to keep on farming. The supervisor told me of another young city woman who joined the Land Army, immediately developed an ambition to own her own milk cows and run a dairy after the war is over, and has saved enough to buy two cows, which her employer allows her to keep on his farm. A lot of the girls brought up on farms prefer working in factories to joining that "Army" with the duties of which they are too familiar.

In common with the rest of the British population, farm people, the younger generation and the new scientific-minded business type of farmer especially, are clamoring for postwar improvements in rural living conditions. Perhaps social-minded city people are clamoring for them louder. There are country slums as well as city slums. Many a village cottage that looks so attractive under its thatched roof, vines on its walls and summer garden embowering it, is comfortless and unsanitary within during many months of the year. Its inhabitants may draw water from a shallow well shared by other cottagers; on stormy nights they have to go "up the garden" instead of to a bathroom; not even rugs, only old sacks, may cover the cold brick floor, and wind under the door lifts these; the light to read the Bible by is a poor kerosene lamp, maybe only a candle. But coming-on women know what plumbing, electricity, kitchen conveniences, washing machines are. Rural electrification by the government has strong advocates. As in America, government electricity is just as good as and often cheaper than corporation electricity. Yet if revolution waited for the conservative British farm folk to make it, the old hen could sit on her china eggs till the cows come home.

A town merchant who retired from business, and bought a farm, retained the help attached to it. Soon after taking possession, he went out one afternoon to discover his shepherd dozing under a bush on the down, the flock grazing around him.

"What are you doing, shepherd?" the town farmer asked, rather sternly.

"Looking after your interests," the shepherd replied.

"That's all very well," the town farmer said, "but I'm not paying you to sleep. You can cut thistles, chop down some of these bushes, make yourself useful in off time."

"Well, I baint a-going to do any such thing," the shepherd replied. "I be studying your interests here, I tell 'ee, same as I allus have fer any master."

And the new master had sense enough to know that he couldn't move the mountain. War prices on produce have made many city men look landward. "Why did you buy it?" a farmer asked a city man up in high income tax brackets who had just purchased a neighboring farm.

"Land won't run away," the man of money replied.

"Yes, but if you work it long enough, you'll damn sure wish you could run away," the farmer observed.

As the Mexican proverb goes, "Every dove has her gall." Still, it's mighty restful to be with people who belong to the good earth. Also, it is restful as well as wearisome to belong to the earth. I think of an English farm hand who was cleaning out a drainage ditch alongside a hedge that his master came up to unseen. The farmer, hearing talk, looked over and saw only the laborer.

"Why, who were you talking to, Sam?" he asked.

"Oh, I didn't know you was anywheres nigh," Sam said. "I was only a-talking to an old toad, asking him how he fared. I see him here ten years ago, the last time I cleaned out the ditch. We be old friends."

American soldiers who become well acquainted with English farm folk, and many on the big air bases out in the country do, are struck with how the people get not only satisfaction but happiness out of little things — a bird, the growth of barley, a sow's protection of her pigs, flowers, the seasoning of a manure pile. The people don't seem driven into rushing after a happiness that money can't buy, even in automobiles and theaters. They seem contented and cheerful and in place. They are restful.

2

A million acres is a good deal of land, even in a ranch — the largest in the United States. It is approximately the extent of the most productive area of Great Britain — "the Fenlands," as they are called, draining into The Wash, a bay on the east coast of England. The Wash used to come much farther inland. Two thousand years ago the Romans put up dikes to hold back tide water. A thousand years later the Saxons made their last stand in these Fens against the Norman conquerors, and William the Conqueror did not get to them until he had built a causeway from one ridge, across the Fen marshes, to an island of high ground the Saxons were holding. For hundreds of years Englishmen have been draining the Fens, turning the courses of rivers, digging wide ditches, mounding high dikes, pumping out water, at first with Dutch windmills, now with turbine engines, reclaiming acre by acre the fertile alluvial soil. The present war's demand for the last ounce of food and the government's all-enveloping control of every acre of earth have forced almost the last plot of fen land into cultivation. Only a spot held by the National Trust as a wild life refuge remains in original vegetation. Drainage has caused the earth to shrink so that the streams now run yards above the land level. In dry seasons the winds blow the fine top soil away. I have seen a blinding Dust Bowl cloud over the Fens. It is only a matter of time till a large part of the area will be as low under sea-level as the Netherlands.

As we drove for fifty miles across the levels, I saw here and there stark tree trunks where no trees have grown for thousands of years. The contraction of the soil brings them upward. When a plow hits one, it is marked for excavation and tractor removal. Oak trunks over a hundred feet long have been dragged out, relics of a succession of forests that flourished as far back as 3000 B.C. The Petrified Forest on the Arizona Desert is not more strange. According to geologists, the sea's coming in destroyed the forests, layering them between deposits of clay. The fallen trees have been preserved by the peat they feed.

In the fields against the road we saw windrows and windrows of potatoes, handy for transportation. This was in February. Last fall the potatoes were gathered and heaped into rows covered with earth and straw for preservation and for crews of men, women and children to uncover and sack. Britain raises enough potatoes not only for her own use but for millions of Allied soldiers. "Eat home-grown potatoes and save on imported wheat."

And here and there over the fields I saw more partridges than I have ever seen anywhere else. They are larger than our bobwhites. Moor hens brought life and interest to a drainage ditch. A kestrel hawk fluttered its wings stationary in the air. What constantly strikes an American is that so much wild life is preserved in a country so densely populated. After Theodore Roosevelt visited England in 1910 he recorded his enthusiasm for the extraordinary way in which — not despite, but because of, the civilized population — the countryside has been preserved. I saw gulls following a plowman, picking up the worms he exposed, and my memory went back to the blackbirds following my father's plow in the field on Long Hollow in Live Oak County. It was a warm winter day, I remember, when I saw the greatest following of blackbirds. They were there in multiplied hundreds. I was so young that I thought it a great privilege to walk along and hold the lines — the horses really needed no guiding —

while my father held the plow handles. He was whistling, and his whistle comes to me now across the years as cheerful as the call of the field lark on the grass.

The name of the farmer in the Fens that we visited is Herbert Carter. His people have been farming for generations. His house, overlooking the River Nen, was lived in at least as far back as 1505. It is provided with modern plumbing and with electricity and is well accommodated to modern life. It and the farm on which it stands have been owned by Trinity College, Cambridge, for three hundred years. Mr. Carter's wife's people rented and operated the farm for generations before Carter himself took it over. Many of the best farmers of this country stay with the same ground as renters for generations, just as generations of farm laborers live in the same cottage and inherit the rights to milk and wood. In ancient days the Carter home belonged to the lord of the manor. I am sure the lord took no better care of it and had no more pride in it than the present mistress and master. The low-ceilinged, snug, restful living room, with cheerful fire and be-at-ease atmosphere, was decorated with belts of horse brasses, once highly prized by men who drove horses, now collected by women who drive bargains with antique dealers.

Carter operates over four thousand acres of land, in scattered parcels. He drove us to a tract of one hundred and sixty acres he purchased about two years ago. It had never within living memory produced a paying crop, was taken with a form of grass more pernicious than Johnson grass. It had belonged to absentee owners and was farmed by a tenant who spent most of his time with gun or fishing rod. Carter has already conquered the wild oats and the pernicious grass, improved the drainage, repaired the barn and cattle sheds, fixed up the farm-worker's cottage, and given an air of thrift and productiveness to the whole farm. I will venture that he could double his money on the purchase.

He led us to pens and sheds where he was feeding three hundred and fifty head of red Lincolnshire steers, most of them three years old, the tops weighing up around eighteen hundred pounds. He did not seem ashamed of a bunch of steers he bought early in the war for ten pounds and sold at sixty-seven pounds. He does not raise cattle or horses; he buys them. He raises hundreds of Essex hogs — a breed designed for bacon and not for lard exclusively. They stand halfway between the lean razorback and those slightly animated barrels called Poland China, Berkshire, and so on, most of the bacon out of which is merely unmelted lard. These Essex hogs strike me as being prime bacon hogs. I hope that Arkansas and other Southern states will never get too progressive to raise plenty of razorback bacon. Progress has made our bread as soft as mush, our butter as hard as a rock, our chicken as fiberless and insipid as spam and a lot of baby beef not much better. It takes muscle to make good meat, and animals too fat to exercise don't develop muscle.

On the average less than twenty-five inches of rain falls annually in the Fen country. The drought of 1944 was preceded by two or three other dry years. The "more cows and less milk" of the old-time West is matched in East Anglia by more dampness and less rain. People used to make "dew ponds" to collect water in. A dew pond is made by excavating a basin and lining the bottom and sides with a blend of clay, lime and straw. There are still dew pond makers; one I have seen a newspaper account of is descended from a family that has been in the business for two hundred and fifty years. He claims to be master of a secret mixture for lining the ponds that will attract dew, cause it to concentrate in the pond. When Mr. Carter spoke of hauling water for stock, I asked him about wells. He said that the coastal Fens are underlaid with salt water. But there are a few fresh water wells, and there are water witches to locate the fresh water. Even if you dig where one of them has located the water, you must dig in the increase of the moon. Dig in the decline of the moon, and you'll get nothing but salt water. Carter wouldn't engage a witch to switch for water; yet if he were going to put down a well, he'd put it down in "the increase of the moon."

I don't know where the Carters get water for their tea. After tramping around in the cold, we got back to the snug parlor on the minute for the most cheering tea, with the best cookies, I ever had. I'd like to sit there, the firelight reflecting on the horse brasses, for a long time and hear Carter tell the lore of the Fens.

The Fens, the Fens! Hundreds of times I have driven across the beautiful Comal basin, on the road between San Antonio and Austin, and I have never looked across from the northern rim of this *comal* (saucer) without seeing in my mind's eye a herd of Longhorn steers, heads up and strung out, striding from the south on their way up the long, long trail to Kansas and Montana. They used to

string over those hills and across that valley every spring
by the tens of thousands. For me their tracks are still on
the hillsides, and the riders beside them still jingle spurs
and search the horizon beyond. And so, somehow, these
Fens of England mirage the passers this way of long ago. I
see the men of the Fens destroying by night the causeway
that William the Conqueror was building by day to reach
their last refuge. Much later I see them resisting organized
movements to drain the Fens and thus to destroy the fish
and eels and wild fowls on which they largely lived. But
to the drainers a tame sheep seemed more valuable than
a wild duck, a bushel of potatoes than a slippery eel.

They don't do anything to celebrate its advent, but the
English have one instrument they cherish as signally as
Americans cherish the Declaration of Independence — the
Great Charter, of 1215. The barons met on the edge of the
Fens to plan to make the tyrant King John recognize their
rights and liberties. The causes leading up to the American
Declaration of Independence lie far deeper in ancient
English demands for liberty, continued for centuries, than
in taxes on tea. After King John had set his seal to the
Charter, he flung himself on the floor and gnawed sticks
and straw and swore by "God's teeth" and by "God's feet."
He set off for Rome and made a new trade with the Pope;
he scurried here and he was harried there in his schemes
to annul the Charter and to re-enact his tyrannies. His last
march was across the neck of The Wash, deep in the Fens.
A tide surprised his forces. Some of his men were lost. All
his baggage was washed away, and with it all the royal
treasures and crown jewels.

The treasure is out there now, under some farmer's beet field, perhaps. Farmer Carter told me that a few years ago an American who claimed to be able to locate gold with "an instrument" got permission to prospect over one of his farms. This American had the backing of capital. He paid good money for the treasure rights on some land. I've always heard that gold sinks six inches — or something like that — every twenty years. If so, King John's jeweled gold is down pretty deep after these seven centuries and more. I'm afraid it won't work up like the skeletons of oak trees that stood in the Fen forests before man had substituted iron for stone or knew what gold would buy. I can look out over the Fens and see King John and his men struggling with pack animals, losing everything they carried — but I can't see where those jewels and gold doubloons are. I don't seem able to dream the right dream.

It is still told in the Fen country how centuries ago a pedlar named John Chapman had a dream bidding him go from his home in Swaffham to London Bridge and there find a pot of gold. The dream came three nights running, and John Chapman was not disobedient to messages he considered heavenly. With his pack and staff and dog he trudged up to London. For three days he poked and ferreted into every possible place on and under London Bridge.

On the evening of the third day an inquisitive citizen who had been noticing his behavior asked him what he was doing. Heartily disgusted by this time, the pedlar told him the whole story of his dreams. "It's nothing but folly," he said.

"Folly, indeed!" the citizen echoed. "Why, if I believed in that sort of dream, I should have wandered off long ago on a wild goose chase to a town called Swaffham in Norfolk. My dream said to go there and find the house of a man named John Chapman and dig for a pot of gold under the apple tree in his garden."

That very night John Chapman set out on the return trip to Swaffham. He dug under his own apple tree; he found a pot of gold. With a part of the gold he built Swaffham Church, and they say that carvings on the bench ends and stained-glass windows used to depict the journey he made with pack, staff and dog to London Bridge and then back to the apple tree with the pot of gold under it.

Living on the edge of the Fens, at Cambridge, I have made several excursions into them and have done more traveling by car in East Anglia than in any other part of England, sometimes going in military cars to army camps, occasionally riding with my agricultural friend Mansfield, when he was on business. I have seldom made a trip in the area without seeing gipsies on the move or camping. After all these war years of government-controlled economy and personal living, the gipsies are still pretty well outside of control. They elude the regional controllers; their ubiquity, even though they are not numerous, is surprising. They remain nomadic horse-traders, horse-doctors, horse-charmers, blacksmiths, palmists, herb-gatherers, rabbit-catchers, mole-catchers, basket-makers, beehive-makers and menders of trifles as they have been for centuries. They still read sign on the ground as expertly as an Apache warrior.

A dozen times at a road crossing between Newmarket

and Bury St. Edmunds I have passed a solitary grave that the gipsies tend. It is enclosed with wickerwork; it always has flowers on it. When I first saw it, crocuses planted on the neat mound were blooming. The grave is about a hundred and fifty years old, they say. One story is that a gipsy hanged for sheep-stealing is buried here. Another story is that a young shepherd hanged himself in despair because somebody else stole some of his sheep, for which he would be accused of stealing; and that his body, in accordance with the church's rules towards suicides, was denied Christian burial and was buried at the crossroads, without benefit of clergy, a stake driven through his heart to prevent his ghost from wandering. Anyway, while tractors imported from America whirr on fields to the right and to the left of this solitary grave at the crossroads, gipsies still keep the grave neat and put flowers on it.

3

I liked Arthur Rickwood, Suffolk farmer, from the moment I laid eyes on him — honest, decisive, direct, simple in the right way. He operates about 8000 acres of scattered farms, owning a considerable portion of the land, renting the remainder. He did not tell me this himself. He did tell me that his father was a farm laborer and that not long before this war started he bought the farm on which he made his first earnings as a boy, leading a plowhorse at a dime a day. He fought in the trenches in the last war and saw comrades drown in the mud of shell craters. After he got back from the war, he resumed farming; and by thrift, good management and industry worked up to be one of the foremost farmers of the British Isles.

I saw machines cutting and digging out trenches as straight as a die to drain his fenlands. I saw tractors and teams harrowing, furrowing, fertilizing, planting upland that three years ago was producing only inferior grass shrub, used principally as covert for pheasants, but that now grows potatoes, beets, parsnips, grain to help feed the nation. Virtually all of his increased profits — and they are large — go into income taxes. That does not deduct from either his enterprise or his pride in making an effective contribution to his country's welfare. Losing money annually on a herd of steers he feeds does not worry him. He can deduct the loss from produce profits; the government, not he, will take the deduction, though, as he says, "this is not business." The steers are fed for the primary purpose of translating vast quantities of straw into muck and manure to be put back into the soil.

Rickwood uses tons and tons of commercial fertilizer annually, but his faith is in nature's fertilizer — organic matter. Perhaps the only way to keep land fertile over centuries of time is to raise stock along with tilling, and to rotate over the ground animals that dung and urinate. Back in the centuries of serfdom, villagers were required to drive their sheep and cattle into the lord's fold at night "in order that his lands might be enriched by the manure." Now that machines are everywhere taking the place of fertilizer-spreading horses and that human food is being grown

instead of forage crops for animals wont to pay the soil
back, many people in England are alarmed over land fertility. Scientists, most of them at least, say that commercial
mixtures of phosphates, nitrates, lime and other ingredients
give the soil all it needs and that if it is consistently treated
with these mixtures, it will not wear out. The people are
not easy, however. An active-minded oil investor halted
me on the street one day to tell me that if his country, along
with mine also, does not, like China, devise a way of turning human sewage into the soil, it will fall, like Rome.

Assertions to the contrary, by scientific agriculturists and
by fertilizer manufacturers through their cohorts of paid
chemists, have left many informed people unconvinced that
commercial fertilizer can take the place of manure. No
commercial fertilizer has the bacteria, so potent in the earth,
of decayed organic matter. To quote from *This Farming
Business*, by Frank Sykes, one of scores of recent books
concerned with the land: "It is argued that plants grown
with the aid of artificial and inorganic manures have not
the same health-giving properties as those drawing their
sustenance from humus alone. We have only just discovered
that man does not live by proteins and carbohydrates alone
and that a whole range of vitamins are essential to the human body. It may be that the plant has similar needs which
are supplied by humus; but as yet there is no indisputable
proof of the theory. . . . If the scientist could analyze a
sample of our soil with sufficient accuracy, and if the many
chemical reactions continually taking place in the living
soil were not so complex, the manuring of crops would become an exact science."

In drawing rooms as well as on farms, in pubs, sewing circles, churches and schools, soil fertility has become something of a cult. I hear of farmers — not cold-blooded scientists — who are burying cow horns north, south, east and west of their manure piles with some sort of idea that the horn will convey the very essence of fertility into the earth-food. This is probably not so effective as a water-sprinkler system for keeping a mammoth compost pile wet that I saw on a farm in Cumberland. The horn burial seems akin to the ancient idea that a dam across a stream will be strengthened by the incorporation of a human body.

What man, woman or boy of the prairies has not seen, year after year, a richer grass with a deeper green grow on the spot of ground where the carcass of an old horse or some cow brute rotted away? I have never buried a dead cat in a bank of earth without expecting a Mexican primrose to blossom richer there.

> I sometimes think that never blows so red
> The Rose as where some buried Caesar bled;
> That every Hyacinth the Garden wears
> Dropt in her Lap from some once lovely Head.

To burn leaves and stalks is certainly as cruel and heartless to the life-sustaining earth as to refuse meat to a man a-hungered. In the "strange, stern justice in the long swing of events," to quote one of Mr. Churchill's lifting phrases, the cremation of the bodies of cattle, men and other animals may be revenged eventually in the ribbed skeletons of beggars mutely pleading for bread that the starved earth cannot yield. Dust to dust. A part of the morality of living in the country comes from the fact that a man may go out daily and return a fragment of fertilizer to the soil he lives on and by.

Few outrages to humanity and to nature are more outrageous than the idiotic practice of those irresponsible rich people who build costly mausoleums in which to preserve their mortician-manicured corpses, the marble that jeers their vanity usurping space on which a lizard might sun himself and in which an earthworm might comfortably digest earth. California, I understand, leads America in this form of idiocy. I hold no brief for any title of nobility, but I doubt if all the history of all the pettiness, snobbery, selfishness and disregard for fellow earth-born creatures comprised in all the English lords that ever lived could produce a single instance so undemocratic as this growing practice of monetary ignobility. At a recent auction in London a Member of Parliament bought for three hundred pounds the Hawley Military Papers. He bought them in order to present them to the Royal Dragoons, of which Hawley was colonel in the eighteenth century. Among the papers was Hawley's will, which he wrote himself "because I have the worst opinion of all members of the law." In this will he directed that "my carcass be put anywhere; 'tis equal to me, but I will have no expense or ridiculous show any more than if a poor soldier (who is as good a man) was to be buried from the hospital. The priest, I conclude, will have his due; let the puppy have it. Pay the carpenter for the box."

4

When I visited the House of Lords, Viscount Bledisloe ("Old Bloody Slow," as he is popularly called) was just beginning a disquisition upon soil fertility, food production, livestock breeds, earthworms. It seemed to me democratic and English to the core that this peer, so deliberate in his manner, honorable for a lifetime of service to agriculture, should be so grave in his concern for his country's soil and other factors concerning the home supply of food that will be as vital to the British people in peace as it has been in war. What was worrying Lord Bledisloe especially is that artificial fertilizer containing sulphate of ammonia is said to check or even totally inhibit the beneficent work of earthworms.

When I went outside on Parliament Square and contemplated the noble statue of Abraham Lincoln sculptured half a century ago by Saint-Gaudens, loftiest of all American sculptors, standing across from the bronzed likeness of that other great liberator, Oliver Cromwell, I felt the harmony of the whole pattern.

There are people in England who would as soon contemplate the loss of their harbors as the loss of their earthworms. Charles Darwin's astounding book on *The Formation of Vegetable Mould through the Action of Worms, with Observations on Their Habits*, first published in 1881, reveals that 53,767 earthworms, weighing 356 pounds, cast up 7.56 tons of earth on an acre of ground in one year, their castings covering it at the rate of .22 inch annually; that the worms generate humus-acids and that their gizzards add to the attrition of hard particles passing through them; that their constant bringing up of soil buries small rocks left on the surface while large stones, undermined by them, slowly sink; that all mould covering a field passes through worm bodies every few years.

W. H. Hudson in his essay "Concerning Lawns and Earthworms," in *The Book of a Naturalist*, tells how a gardener who did not like the sight of worm mounds on his grass starved out the worms by taking away all leaves for them to feed on and then saw his grass spindle away and die, whereas Hudson brought the grass back by feeding the worms. I do not know how the earthworm population of England compares with that of other countries, but it is certainly very high. The worms themselves seem colder-blooded than those in the plots of American earth that I am familiar with. The college quadrangle that I walk around and across several times a day, the grass on it remaining green all winter, is studded in midwinter with earthworm mounds. The worms come out on days severely cold. One raw day I discovered one making his way across flagstones to a rock wall. The poor creature did not know where it was going. I picked it up and put it in the grass so that it could pilot back down to its natural home, but a blackbird probably found it before it had finished its airing.

I wonder if many American farmers are conscious of the extent to which certain national agricultural magazines are run primarily for the profit of manufacturers with machinery to sell. I doubt if British farmers will ever stock up on machinery to the extent that many American farmers stock up on it. I doubt if such stocking up would be to their good. Compared with American milk, English milk is low in butter fat and high in tuberculosis germs. A vast part of the Western Hemisphere is stocked with cattle derived from famous British breeds — Herefords, Durhams, Aberdeen Angus, Jerseys and others; but despite this lead in breeding, the average English farmer's stock is mongrel, often downright scrubby. For going on a hundred years British economy has been run to advantage industrialists at the expense of farmers, food being the currency in which foreign nations have paid for British manufactured goods.

Now, assurances are not lacking that the land will out-produce in quantity and quality all previous peacetime production. A nation convinced that its destiny depends on feeding itself as far as possible is in ferment with ideas about food production. This nation will hardly again legislate for a system of taxes and tariffs designed to enrich manufacturers to the impoverishment of soil tillers. It is not likely to permit entirely free enterprise to city capitalists who would withdraw land — bought to escape taxes and themselves on — from production merely for the delectation of fox hunters and pheasant shooters. Some people will always find a good life on the land. Of course, there is no predicting the extremes of shortsightedness to which economic blocs will go if given free rein. Capable young men are turning to agriculture as they turn to chemistry, their enthusiasm whetted with belief that science may unlock as many not yet discovered riches as the discovery of a new continent unlocked for their Elizabethan forbears. There is a very strong feeling in the English public that man can by knowledge, thought, science, legislation manage soil into more abundance and society into better ways of living. But the land is so little compared with the population.

Dwellers on the soil of the old world seem to feel a loyalty to it, a moral obligation to pay it back, that Americans are only now coming to. Many American soldiers are observing British agricultural methods. A county agent from among them, who gives talks on American farming to women of the Land Army near his base, told me that when he began professional work back home, a farmer said, "Hell, I've wore out more land than that young squirt ever walked over." The Friends of the Soil organization started in Ohio is going to have recruits from the returning ranks.

Make an N. B. of this. Had it not been for landed estates in the hands of old and noble families who have consistently remained responsible to the soil and to society, farming and livestock breeding would have been in a sad state indeed in England. I salute those old dukes who stipulate in their wills that their bodies are to be drawn to the grave in a farm cart — and double-damn the morticians.

CHAPTER IX
The Lark at Heaven's Gate

SOCIOLOGISTS have added many definitions of culture, but to the civilized it always has aroma. "No man," Mary Austin wrote, "has ever really entered into the heart of any country until he has adopted or made up myths about its familiar objects." Myths include carvings, pictures, poems, stories, homely uses, anecdotes, all manner of associations and accretions that make the familiar objects dearer and enhance "affection and reverence" for them. Saint-Martin's-in-the-Fields — and it has been two hundred years since the paved-over fields around Saint Martin's were glad with buttercups — there in the heart of London is still "the parish church of all the world." You'll know when you get to the parish by the little figure on the lampposts of a Roman cavalryman cutting his cloak in two so as to give half of it to a beggar perishing with cold. This "fell about the Martinmas" a thousand and six hundred years ago, but somehow when to the generations of listening children,

"You owe me five farthings,"
Say the bells of St. Martin's,

they seem to be remembering flowers that blossomed in
the dust of fields long before they themselves were
moulded.

I

A lady who gave me some cowslips she had gathered in
the country and brought back to London seemed to be
expressing something incorporated within the flowers,
rather than to be quoting Shakespeare, as she repeated in
her rich voice: —

> The cowslips tall her pensioners be;
> In their gold coats spots you see . . .

In loving the familiar objects of their country, the English
find in them, as no other people find in their own familiar
objects, the accretions of long successions of lovers who
have loved both wildly and wisely. It is not true that "that
which we call a rose by any other name would smell as
sweet." It might have been true in the Garden of Eden,
but now so much of experience and expressed loveliness
inheres in the very word "rose."

> Strew on her roses, roses,
> And never a spray of yew.

"Roses and Fannies and Fannies and roses, thick as leaves
in Vallombrosa," and forever to every lover speaking the
English language will every true love be like a red, red

rose, her mouth a rose itself whose beauty will never ebb, and a rose too in the deeps of his heart. The song of an unknown bird may be very beautiful, but not nearly so beautiful as when for the listener it has incorporated into itself the songs of those who have sung about it.

One early morning in the merry month of May I went out on Grantchester Meadows to hear the skylarks. I was not going merely to hear "a bird" sing. I was going to hear that "scorner of the ground," that "unbodied joy," that "herald of the morn," "messenger of day," the "blithe lark," the "bisy lark," the "holy lark" that Chaucer, Shakespeare, Shelley and so many other poets have for me for so many good years been making to "shake the dew" from its "light wing" as it rises from its ground nest and "at heaven's gate sings," becoming a "sightless song" in the sky while it continues to pour out its "shrill delight." Being the first to discover a continent, to circumnavigate the globe, to climb Pike's Peak, to go down into the Grand Canyon, to send a message by air, to print words, to bring back a description of the Andean condor, to tread where no man had ever trod before, must give a great lift to the pioneer; but if I should among all the measurers of beanstalks come first upon the tallest beanstalk in the world, I should not be so thrilled at locating its latitude and longitude and recording its altitude as at seeing where Jack the Giant-Killer had climbed. That beanstalk would be much more than itself; it would be Jack the Giant-Killer also. Had I gone out to listen to the lark ignorant of all other listeners before me, I know I should have found pleasure in its "sweet jargoning," its "tirra-lirra" out of the dewy air, but I should not have gone again and again, on cloudy, windy afternoons as well as in morning times, to hillsides and the meadows until the larks soaring and singing, dropping their notes like cascades of air-blown silver from perches in the sky, "singing, singing, singing over the wheat fields wide," became a part of my being and enriched the enrichers of their song.

I would not be so absurd as to argue that some fever-consumed English soldier remembering in some jungle of Burma the dear features of his home in the Chiltern Hills, and remembering among those features the skylark, calls up all the poetic lumber that I have called up. With joy but without consciousness of a single poet-enricher, I have a thousand times heard the bobwhite call clear over the mesquite grass at sunrise, the roadrunner go *crut-crut-crut* in the chaparral in the middle of the day, the bullbat zoom down over the prairie at twilight, the querulous little screech owl, who never knows how deliciously funny he is, complain in the gathering darkness, and the wild, long, lonely, lonesome fluting of the southbound sandhill cranes come out of the night. These and many other creatures that add to the song of the corner of the earth in which I have my roots are very dear to me; but often I miss the endowments, the lightings up, the translations of them into the stream of human destiny that only Bards of Passion and of Mirth can give.

Without such, the skylark would be a kind of naked ghost of what the enrichers from Homer's time have been making him. There is no civilization without art; there is no art without the beautiful; half of what is interesting and beautiful lies in accreted memories. "Oh, antiquity, what art thou, being nothing, yet everything!"

The stag at eve had drunk his fill

long before Sir Walter Scott's horses pulled what remained of him to desolated Dryburgh Abbey overlooking the Tweed. Landseer painted stags and modeled lions and passed. But what man who has claimed the inheritance these two left him can ever look at a stag in the Highlands without seeing a wilder and richer beauty because of the line that Scott wrote and the picture that Landseer drew?

A people with the pound sterling and a bulldog for their symbols and flats for homes would never be characterized as artistic. Yet artistic enrichers expressing them have, through words, color, line, gardening, architecture, wrought cumulatively for so long a time that the natural life and physical features of their land seem to have absorbed the art. Poets and storytellers have so come home to and infused flower, bird, bush and down that their art often seems a part of the subject played upon rather than art itself. Multiplied representations of the creatures, from the cricket on the hearth to the raven hoarse with croaking Duncan's fate, have become so familiarly associated with them that they themselves long since became integrated with human life. Here, indeed, we see a culture that "deserves and receives affection and reverence from the people themselves."

When I came to England I knew that though I might not walk on top of the Roman wall, I would with my own ears hear nightingales, cuckoos, skylarks, thrushes, blackbirds

and the chaffinch "on the orchard bough." I knew that I
would see with my own eyes marigolds, cowslips, buttercups, hosts of golden daffodils, the hawthorn hedge in
bloom, the daisy that Burns plowed up, a violet by a moss-
grown stone, and that

> About the woodlands I *would* go
> To see the cherry hung with snow.

Spring opened and it was as if I had been a lover long
wedded to some unseen lovely lady at last about to be
revealed. England in April, and on through May and
June, is all that the crocuses of late winter always promise
and all that all the poets have said it is. The wrongs of the
long, dreary, weary winter are utterly redressed and
blotted out, the unpetaled dimness magicked into sunshine
under which the whole earth greens, flowers and sings.
Lovely by nature, this earth is lovelier because the people
have for so many generations cultivated it through their
spirit as well as with their hands. The standardized "study"
on "the influence of nature" on this or that poet may some
day be varied by one on the influence of poets on nature.
The fields of growing grain and the splotches of native
woods seem turned into parts of a far-spread and in-
finitely various garden. I will set down some of the impressions as they came to me fresh on spring days.

The "rathe primrose" makes me want to tread "the
primrose path of dalliance" clear down to the Valley of
the Doones in Devonshire and see where Lorna's long
dark hair flowed into the primroses at her feet, so that
afterwards as long as he lived John Ridd would never

see them without seeing her standing among them. Avenues of horse chestnuts, their white blossoms standing up like myriads of miniature yucca stalks, are very stately and beds of roses, no matter in what form, always delight, but all such planting reveals the handiwork of man. The yellow primrose that peeps beneath the thorn is surely the most unselfconscious flower that unfolds. No amount of talk about it could ever identify it with man. It is just there, like the infinitesimal atomies that at night illumine a breaking wave on the edge of the world, or like the motes dancing in a sunbeam. Primroses do not, like a host of golden daffodils,

> take the winds of March with beauty.

What is it in their modest loveliness that makes them so dear and makes a human being pausing where they blossom low on the ground feel so gladly serene and so quiet — as quiet as a single leaf drifting downward from an elm tree in October when not a breath of air is stirring? They can be and are transplanted, but it does not seem as if they should be. They seem as almost no other flower to belong where they are. And somehow they make me feel as if I too belonged.

On an April afternoon I went out to a lane lined on either side for about a quarter of a mile with cherry trees all in literally solid snowy bloom. The sun was shining bright not only on but in the blossoms. I got under them and looked skyward and out; I looked up the lane and I went to the end of it and looked down the lane. I don't think I ever saw anything else so fairylike and sheerly beautiful.

It is not that a single cherry flower is more beautiful than certain other flowers; yet each one is very beautiful, and the flowers grow incredibly thick on every stem and branch. No wonder that rows and woodlands of these cherry trees, their white flowers thicker than blossoms in paradise, breathing out a perfume softer than the lowest whisper that lovers ever whispered, make men and women and children of all ages and conditions stand mute with admiration while they want to dance with joy. "Loveliest of trees," surely and most surely it is. Why am I not "far in a western brook-land" where the Shropshire lad looked at "these things in bloom"? If April and I could last forever, I should want at every waking into daylight to rush forth to behold them. And what would they be under full moonlight!

After the cherry trees I went to hear nightingales sing in a tangle of hawthorn beside a stretch of tall woods. I was more eager to hear them than I have ever been to see Rome. They did not disappoint me, in the twilight and then into the darkness. What carrying power their voices have, seeming to envelop the whole air! A timber man tells me that last year a camp of foresters in Surrey were so kept awake by the all-night singing that they moved camp out into a field. I suppose they selected a field a considerable distance away. Chaucer's Squire — "he was as fresh as is the month of May" — slept no more by night than doth a nightingale. The foresters must have all been older than Father William, else the nightingales would have transmuted some of them into sleep-despising squires. It was monasterial Edward the Confessor who grew so sick of the incessant singing of nightingales in the forest where he housed that he prayed heaven to silence them — whereupon they left and did not come back until after he had died.

I doubt if the nightingale song is any more beautiful than that of our Southern mockingbird, which in the spring goes absolutely delirious with the joyful prickings of nature, often springing upward from its high, clear perch as if to race with the song itself and sometimes keeping up the singing the livelong night. There is one glory of the stars and another glory of the moon. The nightingale's song seems to have in it "a richer woe," but perhaps that is because what it pours out into the night air contains so much drawn from listeners of the past. For the most expressive of these listeners, "half in love with easeful Death" — because wholly in love with Life — the "ravished nightingale" "sings on as if in pain." For me, its "jug, jug, jug" adds brightness to woes. To Wordsworth, rightly earthy about so many natural things, its "steady bliss" brought the idea that

> Thou singest as if the God of wine
> Had helped thee to a Valentine.

Anyhow, it seems a waste of time to stay inside while one might be out listening to nightingales.

It is the blackbird that comes nearest to the mockingbird in variety, merriment and long season of song. Charles C. Leel of San Antonio knew the nightingales as a youth in England, and he has written me an interesting note of comparison. "I have," he says, "analyzed the mockingbird's song as compared with the nightingale's. The main difference is that the nightingale's song is all pure flutelike notes, with no exceptions, whereas the mockingbird's is two-thirds of pure and beautiful musical notes, intermingled with one-third of the harshest squeaks and screeches. I reckoned up that percentage, on my fingers, while a mockingbird was singing last night and have found another mockingbird's song to run the same percentage."

2

April in England simply takes possession of human beings, releases them, as it does nightingales. The day after first listening to them I went to a circus in a tent on a grassy meadow called Midsummer Common. There was no dust. The seats were filled with children. All during the performance a little girl kept gathering daisies from the grass in front of my seat. Not far away an American soldier took another little girl in his lap, her pleased mother being in the predicament of the old woman who lived in a shoe. The best act was with a pied horse — not a pinto as we know the color. This horse was spotted all over like a Dalmatian dog, sorrel on white, as Appalusian horses are spotted on the hips. In build he looked like a quarter horse. While he did his tricks, a phonograph played the music for "Las Cuatro Milpas." It swept me back to the summer of 1909 in Chicago when I went to Buffalo Bill's Wild West show. Cooped up in that city, I was sick for space and horses. When I saw Buffalo Bill's Mexican vaqueros dashing about, I ran down against the wire in front of the stand and yelled to them the way vaqueros yell and they yelled back. That was true Mexican music.

There was in this circus on Midsummer Common a little chunky brown mule, about a hand higher than a Texas jackrabbit. The ringmaster offered ten shillings to whoever could ride him, bareback. A hefty girl maybe eleven years old tried two or three times to spring onto his back but she never got more than a leg over his neck; two or three college boys got part way on his neck; then a muscle-legged kid around twelve years old, after a wallow or two on the mule's neck, got a seat behind his shoulders, gripped him with his legs and stayed with him to a fare-you-well while the crowd clapped. I saw him get the ten shillings.

It's fine to have thoughts and philosophies about freedom. An American soldier who asked me what I thought about guaranteeing American prosperity by forcing South American countries to buy all their imported machinery from the United States had not thought at all. The liveliest sensations of freedom I have ever had have come from nature — where I wasn't thinking much of anything, where a horse and I had plenty of space and were free in the same way as the blue quail, the deer and the hawks were free. Cages of rabbits, tortoises, parrots, monkeys and other creatures that show no resentment at being cooped up never interest me.

There were two golden eagles in a big cage in the London zoo. One of them kept spreading his wings as if to take off, looking at the heavy cage-wires, and then not flying. His head had been bruised too often. Both eagles kept turning their heads constantly, looking this way and that way — looking towards a remembered freedom away out in the spaces beyond. An inscription on the cage said that one of them had been in captivity since 1928. Sixteen years of imprisonment, and the instinct for liberty still fiercely burning! It will burn as long as the eagle has life, and that may be for many more decades. As an age-old rhyme has it: —

> Thrice the age of a hound the age of a steed.
> Thrice the age of a steed the age of a man.
> Thrice the age of a man the age of an eagle.
> Thrice the age of an eagle the age of an oak.

This eagle in the London cage was many eagles. In the spring of 1925 the 101 Wild West Show at the Miller Brothers' ranch in Oklahoma had plenty of wild cattle, mostly Brahmas from the Texas coast, pitching horses and riders. They also had the Arkansas River bottom, right by ranch headquarters, full of Indians dressed in native costume. Their tepees were pitched among the open trees along the bank. As my wife and I walked past a certain tepee a little apart, an old warrior came out of it and stood facing the river. In the water below him two Indian youths were fooling with a *put-put-putting* motor boat. Immense in frame, though *gastado* (spent) as the Mexicans say, the old warrior stood there, utterly ignoring the crowds and in gutturals uttering curses not loud but deep on all machines and the people of machines that had taken away the free lands, the free game, even the free air he had been born to. I never saw on any other man's face such a gazing into the lost past, such a hatred of the imprisoning present, or heard — though in an unknown tongue — such intense curses of mingled pride and yearning. I did not rightly comprehend him until we walked on and came to an eagle in a cage in front of the ranch store.

The eagle had not been there many weeks, I judged. Its head was bloody from flights against the wiring, but as unbowed as the spirit of Lucifer. Ready to spring from its stout perch, the great imprisoned bird of freedom was not still for a second. Constantly, with energy that was heart-breaking, it becked its head to the right and to the left and almost clear around to the rear, while the wild, yellow eyes searched for an opening into the sunlit air that waited limitless all above and beyond. A thousand times since I have wished that I had gone into the store and bought a pair of pliers and cut the heavy wires. If those eagle eyes saw the gawking human beings for whose degraded delight it had been imprisoned, they saw with a curse more horrible than that in a dead man's eye. And in them was all the fierce lust for liberty that only the soarers know and only the soarers when caged remember.

Once at a roadside joint in Gonzales County, Texas, I saw a coyote very rapidly trotting up and down his long-ish, narrow cage. I stood still in front of him. While he trotted, trotted, whirling at each end of his little runway, he was looking past me, past everything, away and away out. I watched him for maybe fifteen minutes, during which time he never slackened his pace, not even when turning. Then I went and asked the man who sold the bellywash at the joint how long the coyote had been caged.

"Twelve years," he answered.

"And he has never become a vegetable, resigned to the cage?"

"Never."

I never saw grass so green anywhere else as this April grass in England, dandelions so handsome. Orchards all in bloom. Walkers on the road with cowslips in their hands. An old Englishman full of memories said to me, "I know Japan very well. It is lovely, but not so lovely as England is now. Maybe it's the Japanese people. They have no sense of humor, no play in them."

3

In March I had felt that a Peer interested in earthworms made a pattern with Lincoln and Cromwell. As I walked on down to Saint James's Park that day and saw the birds in the water and people feeding them, the pattern became clearer. At this time of year the birds are principally a mixed variety of ducks, along with gulls, moor hens and pelicans. At the bridge over the little lake, a plain, solid-standing, middle-aged woman who had manifestly done hard physical work most of her life was feeding sparrows on the railing and pitching crumbs to the ducks in the water. She was getting a great deal of pleasure taking the crumbs, bit by bit, out of a worn leather bag and impartially portioning them.

When she saw me standing by and sharing her pleasure, she said, "I think they are coming to know this old bag." Then she added, "It isn't really waste, you know. I don't bring anything but the leftovers. Nobody would eat what I am giving the birds. I wouldn't waste food." Now, trying to catch a bite before it reached the water, the white gulls scooped through the air, one of them often lighting on the back of one of the clustered ducks! How the diving ducks dived! How the green on the heads of the India ducks glistened! How quiet the sparrows were, even daring to take food from the feeder's hand! After the last crumb from the old bag had been dispensed and the birds were scattering to find another benefactor, I said to this woman, "I want to thank you for myself as well as for the ducks." And with a smile she went her solid way and I went my way.

That way was up to Trafalgar Square, where as always somebody was feeding the pigeons. A pedlar was selling little packages of a kind of pea. Mothers were buying the peas for their little ones to feed the pigeons. A photographer was snap-shotting an American sergeant and his girl holding out handfuls of peas with the pigeons lighting on their hands and wrists and pecking the food up. Then two lads in R.A.F. blue had their pictures made together with the pigeons alit on and fluttering about their hands.

According to the last official count, or estimate, of the birds in Britain, there were close to a hundred million — ten million chaffinches, four million sparrows, with blackbirds, robins, and thrushes close runners-up. There must be more birds in England than in any other developed and civilized land of its size on earth. It isn't just that they find refuge and feed in the gardens of town and country and the hedges that divide the plots of land and in the woods, or that the land's productivity favors them as no other land. It isn't just that. There are hardly any birds, comparatively, in France. They were killed out long ago. The English people cherish birds as creatures that add to the interest and charm of life. They cherish them and protect them also as economic destroyers of insects and rodents hostile to produce. For two weeks or more *The Times* has been printing letters from over the country for and against the "little owl," which seems to be not an unmitigated blessing but which evidently has more friends than enemies. It is the same with the badger, debated extensively, in newspaper letters. The attitude towards birds is a part of the pattern that harmonizes peers and earthworms; the embronzed immortals on Parliament Square and little sparrows; the bold ducks and the plain woman in Saint James's Park; the children and the pigeons and the lovers and the admiral with the "soul of a North Sea storm" on Trafalgar Square; and the little owl and the unassembled parliament of citizens over this old and beautiful land who debate his case.

The Old Roman Road I walked down on a day in June has for generations been one of the many "grass paths" that preserve savor in this country for travelers on foot. Fields of barley sloping up to its straight over-the-hills course waved like a soft sea. Over it skylarks crisscrossed swallows and swifts. Beside it I learned the little blue flower called "speedwell" and the wonderfully aromatic wild thyme. Now,

I know a bank whereon the wild thyme blows.

Kipling called it "dawn of paradise" — from the smell, I guess.

Along a crooked side lane that went a crooked mile, wild roses, the "unofficial flower of England," were all in bloom in the hedges.

All Saint's Hall, by Creeting St. Mary, in Suffolk, has been a kind of home to me. In front of the house is a hollow oak with owls in it. I have stood in the garden so charming and homey and counted hundreds of planes flashing in the sun on their way to German destruction. Out back is a pond, where I saw my first moor hen nest. It was near the bank in briars. Later the moor hen built a second nest on a little island of willow branches right out in plain view. I wish somebody would introduce the moor hen into America. It has a charm and, with alternating shyness and indifference to bipeds, a kind of affinity for humanity that the gallinule, its nearest American approach, lacks. To see the little ones scampering over lily pads is as refreshing as cedar waxwing politeness. Every pond and ditch in the country has its moor hen.

By the pond at All Saint's Hall I saw my first chaffinch nest, built low on the bole of a big willow and camouflaged with lichens pasted on the nest. The first "wandering voice" of a cuckoo I ever heard was at this place, and in a ditch through a stretch of Fen I found three little lapwings that played as dead as any possum while their distressed mother made her distressing cries. Around the place I picked cowslips, marsh marigolds, buttercups, bird's eye, lamb's parsley (Queen Anne's lace), ragged robin, and a dozen other wild flowers. I remember two women in the afternoon sunshine putting flowers on graves in the old green churchyard. Here in the larches, the ashes, the oaks, the elms, the willows and the shrubbery the birds seem always to be singing while the fleets of bombers and fighter planes roar towards destiny. I am in a world of drama that is terror itself and I am as utterly away from the world as the bees in the lavender blossoms.

Eighty-five per cent of the English population live in towns and cities, not counting the little groups of farmhouses called villages. Eighty-five per cent of the land is country. There are millions in the cities who would hardly know a hawk from a house wren, but a remarkable number of the audible part of the population seem to have country-going instincts. In Texas I feel hemmed up unless I'm ten miles away from a country post office. I do not understand how I can feel so out and free in a twenty-acre woodland of England, a half-dozen pied wagtails flitting on the lawn of King's College courtyard affording as much relief from human constriction as a remuda of dun horses galloping across a prickly pear flat in the middle of a hundred thousand acres of unpeopled chaparral and mesquite. I have never observed that the owner of many thousands of acres of land loves its features any more or gets any more virtue out of it than the cultivator of a mere plot. When America was stampeding west, Henry David Thoreau remarked that he had not yet explored sufficiently the territory between his front gate and the door step. He did move out a mile or so to Walden Pond, and there saw more of nature than any hunter of the millions of aboriginal buffaloes on an empire of pristine land has left any indication of having seen.

When Thomas Bewick, the eighteenth-century woodcut artist of natural history, set out at the age of fourteen from his little farmland home near the Scottish border, "My heart," he says, "was like to break. As we passed away I inwardly bade farewell to the whinny wilds, to Mickley bank, to the Stob-cross hill, to the water banks, to woods, and to particular trees, and even to the large hollow old elm, which had lain perhaps for centuries past on the haugh near the ford and had sheltered the salmon fishers while at work there from many a bitter blast."

On an American pilot's table in a Nissen hut near the English coast I found a copy of Alice Duer Miller's *The White Cliffs*, and for the first time read it. One sonnet seemed to sum up something far back of the landscape.

> The English love their country with a love
> Steady and simple, wordless, dignified;
> I think it sets their patriotism above
> All others. We Americans have pride —
> We glory in our country's short romance.
> We boast of it and love it. Frenchmen, when
> The ultimate menace came have died for France,
> Logically as they lived. But Englishmen
> Will serve day after day, obey the law,
> And do dull tasks that keep a nation strong.

Once I remember in London how I saw
Pale, shabby people standing in a long
Line in the twilight and the misty rain
To pay their tax. I then saw England plain.

I have been talking with eighty-six-year-old G. G. Coulton, who has probably written more truth about the Middle Ages than any other historian. Eighty-six years old, and he begins his autobiography with an adaptation of one of Shakespeare's sonnets: —

To me, fair *Earth*, you never can be old,
For as you were when first your eye I eyed,
Such seems your beauty still. . . .

I am dead certain that the love of the English for the "fair Earth" and for the growing and flying and running and crawling and standing things on it is enormously responsible for their fixed and unwavering character.

CHAPTER X
Gardens under Bombs and Spires

Go down to Kew in lilac-time, in lilac-time, in lilac-time;
Go down to Kew in lilac-time (it isn't far from London!).

EVERY TIME I've heard an old-fashioned barrel organ playing on a street in London, and I have heard several, I've expected to hear it play out Alfred Noyes's lines about "lilac-time." I'll always listen to a barrel organ, an accordion, a French harp or a guitar; the Fiddler of Dooney could lead me to Jericho, and the Pied Piper of Hamelin to the farthest hill on the other side of Far Away. On a July night in London I slept almost none. It wasn't the pilotless bombs that kept me awake; I had to get up so very early tomorrow in order to make a broadcast that would be heard yesterday night in America. In the hour before dawn, and summer's dawn comes very early in the north countree, while I looked at moonlight's magic on walls bombed to ruins years ago in this long, long war, I knew I would go down to Kew Gardens.

I

Lilac-time was past, but I do not know how any two hundred and eighty-eight acres could be more beautiful at any time than the Royal Botanical Gardens at Kew were when I saw them. It was a warm day, so warm that at noon I took a nap on the grass. Clouds were low and thick, though broken in places, constantly shifting; and the Alert was on in London and the deadly drone of an unliving plane with its burden of destruction could be heard before I left the main part of the city.

You can hear I know not how many miles away that drone which you know will die, and then you hear it die, you hear the silence, and next the explosion. You will not thank God that it blasted out the soul or the home of some other living being; you can hope that it hit in a field, a park, in water; you feel grateful that it passed you by. You have heard thousands of other planes, singly and in armadas of inexorable destiny; and though a machine can have no soul, you have become accustomed to regarding those machines of the sky as personifications of men, young men bright with life, mostly young men of your own blood and tongue. They throb, they drift, they shatter the air as they shoot through it, controlled by skilled human hands. The living made them, the living guide them; they live to assert humanity's right to live free.

But this strange, lone machine in the sky that cannot veer or check until its swift clock has run down, moving without a hand to guide it and without a life to share its destruction, has a sound different from all other sky-cleavers you have ever heard. It is not even manned by a ghost, as was the specter-ship the Ancient Mariner saw moving without sail or oar while the red setting sun shone through her ribs. If all the blood were pumped out of the arteries and veins of a corpse, and then water were kept circulating through them and the unpulsing heart by a hydraulic pump, a stethoscope listener to the circulation would hear a beat as unlike that of a healthy pulse as the throb of a pilotless plane is to that of a life-piloted one. The old charwoman was right. She preferred the blitz to the doodlebugs — "it seemed so much more natural." After you have heard numbers of these machines, you know that you will not take their sound for the living sound; yet you find that imagination may translate the living into the dead, for

> . . . in the night, imagining some fear,
> How easy is a bush suppos'd a bear!

By the time I reached Kew Gardens, the All Clear had sounded. I walked through roses, grass and trees, and came to a lake, beside which a tall, slender old man with a short moustache and a long look in his eye was feeding bread crumbs to a swarm of house sparrows. "English sparrows," we call them in America; just "sparrows," they are generally called in England. A chaffinch, dressed as gallantly as Little Lord Fauntleroy, was trying to get a crumb, but was too genteel in his nature to become part of the mob. The old man pitched him something apart. He also fed a half-dozen half-grown mallard ducks and their mother, also a moor hen, in the water. Three middle-aged women in some sort of home-services uniform, each with a lunch wallet, watched him for a while. He told them that the last time he had been in the gardens he was with his daughter, and a duck they had fed followed them along the gravel walks for half a mile. "It was on a Sunday and there were crowds," he said. "Now a hen will lose her head and get excited in traffic, but a duck keeps as calm as a cork when there ain't no wind, no current and no fish in the water. That duck she just keep waddling at my heels, and I says to my daughter, 'Did ye ever see anything like it?'"

After the three women went on, I spoke to the old man. Thereafter for about forty-five minutes I didn't have to do anything but listen. He'd come out to Kew, he said, to get some peace. The night before a pilotless bomb had exploded all the windows out of the house he lived in. I asked him if it had done much destruction; he said he didn't know, that he didn't look for the place where it landed, didn't want to add to human morbidity. He had been bombed out during the great blitz, but had no idea of leaving London. He was seventy-six years old and had a job — messenger in a government office. "This is your day off, I suppose," I said. "No, I have a two weeks' vacation, and to tell you the truth I don't know what to do with myself."

Yet he was no cockney. He had spent most of his life on the sea. "You don't come from Galveston?" he asked. "I'll never forget that place. Me and another sailor, we was young then, deserted a ship there and got arrested in

Houston. They put us in jail and there we stayed for two weeks. It was the dirtiest jail I was ever in and had more rats. They'd run over you at night. Look at that guard over there after that goose. Geese are bad about pulling up grass. There are generally some blue tits in this hedge. They are the prettiest little birds in the fields."

He got to telling me about a pet blackbird he once had. No, it wasn't kept in a cage. It would fly anywhere and would "sing like one o'clock." For eighteen years it was a family pet. Its old yellow bill turned as white as a parson's collar. One morning when his wife went to the kitchen she heard the old fellow make a peculiar sound. "What's the matter, Jim?" she asked him. He flew to her hand and perched and then turned as dead as a mackerel, just that quick and that easy. He hadn't been sick at all that anybody could tell. Birds die that way, just live on till they quit living, no one-foot-in-the-grave lingering on for them. Then there was a pet magpie. He could talk like all Widdicombe. The man my bird-lover bought him from, for ten bob, did not know he could talk. He'd say, "Come on, Joe, old boy, let's be going." He was great friends with a thrush, and when the thrush died, he grew so restless and miserable and moped so that my friend took him to the zoo, where he could be associated with other birds and where his talking delighted streams of children.

The man of pet birds told me how when he was a boy a market in London used to sell chaffinches that had had their eyes burned out with a red-hot wire point; they sing better in the dark, nothing distracting them. That kind of cruelty was outlawed long ago. Boys don't rob nests as much as they used to and destroy nestlings. Country boys seem worse than city boys. He used to see singing contests between caged chaffinches. The cages, draped with black cloth so as to keep out the light, would be placed in a room. One chaffinch would start up and then they'd be singing against each other like all forty.

This bird-lover had had dogs too, one especially that was a natural-born thief, always stealing out of butcher shops and market baskets, even when he was too full to eat. He was a regular kleptomaniac.

While we — he, rather — talked, the siren went again. Soon we could hear the noise of the pilotless plane. We both looked up into the sky. He looked down a path leading towards the garden lunchroom. "It was right here," he said, "that that duck began following me and me daughter. Did you ever see anything more independent than a duck waddling when she knows exactly where she wants to go?"

Now it was "cheerio" and each went his ways. The pilotless bombs were sporadically straying over. They didn't seem to be predestined to come down to Kew this time. I went through the rock garden, where I found the heather always planted in such places. While I was walking on grass beside a bed of blooming dahlias, the nearest-sounding of all the bombs rushed along. I noticed two bumblebees in the dahlias. There was no sunshine, but they were making hay. In a cloud break I caught a distinct view of the plane. It was still going horizontally, droning that ashes-to-ashes-and-dust-to-dust drone. The bumblebees took no notice of it. I thought of the character I had recently parted from. He was a philosopher and in a different cate-

gory from a pair of only very slightly aware-of-bombs
lovers over in grass under a tree.

When, about one o'clock, I got to the lunchroom, I
saw many tables on the lawn and people at the tables.
The youngest ones seemed more engaged in feeding the
hordes of sparrows than in feeding themselves. Everybody
had to get his own tray of food, cafeteria style, inside. The
house looked to be made half of glass and half of wood.
Just as I got to the entrance, a seedy-featured man with
a far from fresh apron on screeched out, "Take cover!
Take cover!" He flattened out up close to the glass-wooden
wall. I looked at the people at the tables and saw that
nobody paid the least attention to this officious, and perhaps
official, adviser. The pilotless plane certainly did sound
about directly overhead. In a very short time the aproned
man, who looked as if he had not been sleeping much or
eating much either, appeared again. "That one's going to
London sure," he announced. Plenty of its predecessors
had come down on Kew in lilac-time — it isn't far from
London.

There was no sunshine, but the ground was as warm as
the air. Again it was All Clear. I found me a little opening
of springy grass, surrounded by trees — an opening about
big enough to stake two horses on. I could see in all di-
rections from my pallet. I pulled my hat over my eyes and
went to sleep. When I awoke a kestrel hawk was hanging
in the air not far away. It was very beautiful. I walked
by a longish lake and saw three American soldiers trying
to Kodak a pair of foreign-looking geese. I had saved half
my luncheon bread for useful purposes. A bit of it brought

the geese into proper position. Eight children and their mothers came up to enjoy the geese. I threw the last of my bread into a small pond near by covered with water lilies. It was joy to see a moor hen and her three little ones run over the big lily pads. I went on down to the Thames River and walked up it, watching slow barges laden with coal, lumber and other goods being towed by. The men on the barges and boats all seemed interested in the shore life, just as scattered spectators like myself seemed interested in the river life. The river men often pointed to something they saw ashore; they seemed to be a living part of, however separated from, the trees and meadows along both banks.

I rode back to London on top of a bus, well forward. I saw fresh debris being carted down side streets, a pitiful pile of furniture beside one unit of demolished walls and homes. I saw people looking and talking, talking about the pilotless bombs and their work. Like the bombers that were going to conquer England by cowing the people, these only fortify their souls. They will never destroy the character that the bomb-makers hate. Meanwhile the bumblebees in the dahlias, the wood pigeons so gentle in the gardens though they are always wild and wary elsewhere, the duck that follows a man and his daughter for half a mile, hoping for another mouthful, the children feeding birds, the barges on the water, the trees on the banks, the kestrel in the air and the chaffinch in his gay coat on a bough: these will always be new, always refreshing.

Kew in lilac-time, it isn't far from London.

2

A dear friend took me to the nine-acre garden belonging to a Cambridge character. He was in it wearing a sombrero wide enough to shade a horse. A big slash of the garden is now in vegetables; natural woods enclose it; wild flowers and grass brighten at ease the spaces of former flower beds and trimmed lawn. The lupin stems in one remaining bed took my heart a-gallivanting to the lakes of bluebonnets in Texas; the promiscuous cowslips and buttercups filled me with joy. When the owner said something, not complainingly, about war taking gardens back to the wilderness, I told him to read the last essay in W. H. Hudson's *The Book of a Naturalist*. The essay begins: —

I am not a lover of lawns; on the contrary, I regard them, next to gardens, as the least interesting adjuncts of the country-house. Grass, albeit the commonest, is yet one of the most beautiful things in Nature when allowed to grow as Nature intended, or when not too carefully trimmed and brushed. Rather would I see daisies in their thousands, ground ivy, hawkweed, and even the hated plantain with tall stems, and dandelions with splendid flowers and fairy down, than the too-well-tended lawn grass.

The college garden wherein I renew myself several times a day has delighted me all spring because labor is too short to keep the daisies and dandelions down. It would be a terrible prison to me in the immaculate trimness of peace-time. It is frequently too curried down, trimmed up and

confining anyhow, but I think only one of the Fellows
ever misses the naturalness of nature. W. H. Hudson goes
on: —

It appears to me that the idea of lawns, like the idea of
clothes, has entered into our souls, and manifests itself more
and more in all our surroundings, our dwellings, our persons,
our habits. Sir Almroth Wright cried out a little while ago
against our habit of scrubbing our bodies every day and rubbing them dry with rough towels to polish them and make
them shine like glass, china, and plated tableware. When
Nathaniel Hawthorne came to the Old Home from an out-
landish United States of America where this idea of the lawn
had not yet [about 1850] penetrated so deeply, he spent some
time at a great country-house where he stayed in running
about the lawns and park in search of a nettle, or weed, or
wilding of some kind to rest his eyes on. The novel smooth-
ness and artificiality of everything made him mad.

Hudson, as most people who read natural history know,
was reared on the vast-spreading pampas of South America
with wild-riding gauchos, came to England when he was
about twenty, and spent the remainder of a long life remembering, while making many fresh observations, the
pristine spaces he had left. It is not without significance that
he took his stand at Land's End in Cornwall, on the most
southwesternly spot of England. After he was gone, the
inhabitants plaqued a certain seat: "W. H. Hudson used
to sit here." That is fame. His friend was Cunninghame
Graham, also of the Spaces — which the word *Pampas*
means — lonely and immense. Nobody else in the English
tongue has pictured Plains Indian, Arab, Cossack, Cowboy

or any other free rider as Hudson and Graham have presented the Gaucho.

With this idea of the freedom of Spaces always burning inside him, Cunninghame Graham once asked Hudson: "How many men of cultivation, education, and the rest, have seen the Pampa, prairie, desert or the steppes, and putting off the shackles of their bringing up, stayed there for life and become Indians, Arabs, Cossacks, Gauchos; but who ever saw an Indian, Arab, or wild man of any race come of his own accord and put his neck into the noose of a sedentary life and end his days a clerk?"

Graham was a superb horseman and had money for horses, which Hudson did not have. In London parks he used to ride Pampa, an Argentine blaze-faced black that with sweeping tail tossed his mane and pawed the earth, "proud of his pride." One day Hudson rose from his seat in the park when Graham rode up, patted the horse, said, "Oh, Pampa!" put his arms around his neck and wept. Hudson must have been a difficult fellow. Some people down in Cornwall once asked Hudson if they could do anything for him while he was in their vicinity. "Yes," he said, "I'd like to come into your garden to see the birds." He came frequently, but if while he was there any of the household entered the garden, he would emphatically tell them to go away and quit scaring the birds. One day he walked by a bed of tulips and knocked the flowers off with his cane. "What in the devil does anybody want to plant those things for?" he asked. Something of artificiality about the bed and lawn, perhaps also about the people, had no doubt made him boil. Many and many a Hudson among the English has gone out into the great Spaces of the Earth and never come back to lawns.

His neighbors' smoke shall vex his eyes, their voices break his rest.

I go with the Space-lovers. Many times I have thought civilization a sorry refuge from life. Still, I guess I am civilized, and if you have to live in confines instead of in Spaces, there is nothing else like a garden. The ideal life is that of a civilized man with perspective, love of art and gusto living in a fairly bountiful wilderness sparsely peopled with savages. Frederick Ruxton, Englishman, and Cunninghame Graham, Scotsman, realized the ideal better than any moderns I can think of. Almost no American frontiersman had the perspective. Nature is supreme in two aspects: in a wild pristine state unmarred by man, the forest primeval, the sea of grass, mountains timbered and streamed unscarred by road, axe or smoke, the wilderness before Christians have "redeemed" it; then in a state of cultivation that only loving care, good taste, skill, science and rooted humanity can give it. Land that has been exploited but not yet cultivated for graciousness lacks all the freshness and release that nature gave it, has nothing of the charm and delightfulness that humanity can give it. And so for freedom and pleasance, I'll take a hedged-in cottage and its plot anywhere in England rather than many thousands of acres from which the grass that the buffaloes once grazed has all been destroyed and nothing but dollar wheat planted.

3

I have been to Oxford, harboring for three days in the easy hospitality of Exeter College. I didn't go to compare Oxford with Cambridge: I couldn't. I went to make a talk and let what would seep into me. With the exception of one other feature, the gardens seeped deepest — great trees, lawns, flowers, walks, the river, all blending with the ancient walls that belong like oaks, the spires, the sky. Punts with the young and the yare were in the river by Christ Church Meadow, and cows were on the grass; there must have been fifty half-grown wild ducks in a pond in University Park. Addison's Walk, named for the serene philosopher, in the ample gardens of Magdalen College, winds around a deer park in which spotted fawns lifted their ears and nostrils when I whistled — and I felt far away and free. New College is old, old and its garden is not big but it flowed into me like the songs of larks. What is beautiful is true, and had Oxford through the centuries created nothing else but its gardens, it would have added supremely to the spirit of man.

I walked away from the streets where the colleges and the town blend and away from modern streets where there are no colleges. I wanted to get on to the river, the Thames, and out into the country. I passed the commons, where anybody can graze his beast, and saw maybe two hundred cattle and horses. I liked especially a chunky little dun mare with a line down her back — a "bayo coyote" we would call her at home — that was grazing by the towpath along the river. It was Sunday and two children, watched by their father and mother, were trying to walk up to the dun mare's colt. I passed a lock that was opening for two little boats of sails and oars. I came to The Trout, a public house where sporting Oxonians drank ale in Elizabethan times. It is full of old pictures and prints, none of them resembling the "barroom nudes" that are so conventional in American drinking places and that are imitated in officers' bars in American camps over here.

The Bodleian Library is ranked as second only to the British Museum. I went there to try to find out something about the English writer known only as Captain Flack who wrote *The Texas Ranger* and another book about early pioneer life and the wild animals. I had to go through a small formality in order to get into the working part of this great library, but once in, all the keys and unlockers were at my disposal. The librarian said they made it difficult for people without real business so that they could make it easy for people with real business. I do not consider this undemocratic. Like many other British institutions, the Bodleian has in adopting certain modern techniques preserved much of the obsolete. It is always hard to weld wood with steel; yet in a way the English do it.

I went to Rhodes House, headquarters for Rhodes scholars. It seemed a fine place to me for a young scholar to sit and read Thomas Jefferson and dream of immortality — and then walk in the gardens under its windows. It is the Rhodes scholarships that have so advertised Oxford beyond Cambridge in America. In England and over the rest of the civilized world there is no such disparity of fame.

Lytton Strachey said that there are three proper places in the world in which to read mystical and majestical Sir Thomas Browne: floating down the River Euphrates, sitting between the feet of the Sphinx, or retired in the cloisters of Oxford. Lingering in these cloisters, one might remember back to time before antiquity began and forget that the century of the common man ever tried to get born. Actually, habiting here, young men have made Oxford the mother of "movements" to enlarge the spirit of mankind.

The world reserves its high epithets, like Great Emancipator and El Libertador, to men who brought physical freedom. Wandering in the shadows of Oxford's halls, I felt like saluting her as one of the great Liberators, one of the great Emancipators, of the last thousand years of civilized life. During the World Wars, I have not wished Germans slaughtered and sent to hell merely because I feared they would scorch my part of the green earth. Much as I love the greenness of the earth, it is not the limit of my inheritance. The Germans have been out to exterminate a civilization, with all its graces, humanity, imagination, humor, poetry, sense of values, accumulations of what is beautiful and noble, its associations with ten thousand things like Tintern Abbey, London Bridge, Mother Goose, Mr. Pickwick, Alice in Wonderland, Doctor Johnson's name on the painted hem of Mrs. Siddons's skirt, Mercutio's jest, Falstaff's gusto; the sweetness out of calm strength as Big Ben strikes the hour of nine, Colonel Newcome's "*Adsum*," Robin Hood under the greenwood tree, the

Great Charter of Liberties, Elia's puns and withheld tears, the King James translation of the Holy Bible, Bob Cratchit's Christmas Dinner, Queen Mab, cowslips in April, Sir Roger de Coverley's "roast beef stomach," the footprints in the sand that Robinson Crusoe saw, the cloak that Great Raleigh spread on the mud, Cromwell's cutting off the tyrant's head, Charles the Second's apology at dying, the dream that John Bunyan dreamed, Mister Punch, the sermon that John Wesley preached, Chaucer's "nyne and twenty sondry folk" in Tabard Inn, the House of Commons, Sir Philip Sidney's gallantry, the melancholy Dane — who was as English as the ghost that came to him — Milton's voice in the cause of free speech, Nelson's order, Walpole's wit, Burke's indictment of Warren Hastings, the seer of that "light that never was, on sea or land," "the Blue Boy," Little Red Riding Hood, the Society for the Prevention of Cruelty to Animals, Shelley's supernal lines on "The Cloud," Lawrence of Arabia's extravagances, Churchill's promising "nothing but blood, toil, sweat and tears." If civilization were electric refrigerators, it would make no difference who makes our songs or our laws either. How any American who loves the civilization imbedded in the language he speaks could ever stand indifferent or neutral towards a Germany trying to destroy that civilization is beyond my comprehension.

My first hour in Oxford I went to see the figure of Shelley at University College. That "pardlike spirit" of mingled gentleness and fire came there when eighteen, wrote a tract "On the Necessity of Atheism," and was promptly expelled. Schools are for ordinary human beings; genius is at home nowhere. Shelley would have been Shelley had he never seen Oxford. In many ways he was still a child when at the age of thirty, in 1822, he drowned off Italian shores. Towards the end of the century the naked figure of white marble, upheld on bronze wings of the Poetic Muse, was presented to the college that had expelled him. You can see that his hair is still wet from the sea. Death has only enmarbled the symmetry of the most beautiful of young men. A plaque with no other words has these lines from his own *Adonais:* —

> He has out-soared the shadow of our night;
> Envy and calumny and hate and pain,
> And that unrest which men miscall delight,
> Can touch him not and torture not again;
> From the contagion of the world's slow stain
> He is secure, and now can never mourn
> A heart grown cold, a head grown grey in vain —
> Nor, when the spirit's self has ceased to burn,
> With sparkless ashes load an unlamented urn.

Shelley gave Oxford more than it gave him. Yet in the way that great abiding institutions transmute and transmit, Oxford now gives Shelley. In the early morning I went back to look again upon the marble. I felt thankful that it is there for young men of the generations to see.

4

The Ministry of Information had asked me if I would go to Dunmow in Essex on Sunday to take part in an Anglo-

American drumhead service. We drove over low hills golden with August shocks of wheat, barley and rye curing in the just-right sunshine. Against the town we came to a green pasture wherein a platform had been erected and seats placed. Soldiers, both American and British, were marching with flags to positions, and citizens, little girls and big girls in bright dresses, were streaming to the seats. The music was by a Salvation Army band. All the soldiers and a majority of the civilians sat on the grass, twenty-five hundred souls.

The band, military men at attention, played "The Star-Spangled Banner" and "God Save the King." As always, when I hear our national anthem, my imagination went back to days when I had a right to give the military salute and when it seemed to me we were waging a war that would end in a better world. And it would have been a better place if the humanity-betraying reactionaries, the greedy high-tariffers, the boomers of trivialities, the Normalcyites with eyes in the backs of their heads instead of forward, had not had their way. There on the green grass, rimmed by green trees and overtopped by the cloud-flecked blue, the war and the hopes of a quarter of a century ago all flooded back into my memory.

Chaplains prayed the stately prayers of the Church of England. One of them, tall, gray-headed, face chiseled by thought and kindness, preached a sermon hardly ten minutes long. He quoted a chaplain out of the last war who said that sometimes he would have preferred to hear soldiers swearing rather than whining out prayers for little personal favors. "God is never a means," this gray-headed speaker said. Some people might not understand that saying. Let them reflect on politicians who use churches to get votes, on merchants who use the cloak of religion to get customers, on thugs like Goebbels and Hitler who call on God to justify their conduct, on little graspers who advertise themselves, often in big magazines, as being the instruments of divine purposes.

✓ I looked at the men of two nations there on the beautiful grass in the quiet sunshine listening to the quiet wisdom. It seemed to me that "authentic tidings of invisible things" might be flowing into all of us. I realized the impatiences and prejudices that individuals in each uniform might bear for the opposite nationality. At the same time, considering how well our nations have fared with each other for a hundred and thirty years now, how well we fight together, how we are joint heirs of the noblest civilization formed since Christ walked on earth, it was almost incomprehensible to me — at the moment — that we should not be partners.

✓ After the services I met civilians and soldiers. A woman asked me if I do not feel proud of American soldiers; I told her I always feel proudest when I feel the respect for them and the good will towards them that so many citizens of this country bear. A corporal from New York State was not strong on Ham Fish, "the fishiest-smelling ham inside the pork barrel." A sergeant said it was all right to change horses in the middle of the stream but bad to swap a horse for a pony anywhere. From the way two or three other soldiers laughed, I understood this is an army joke.

We went to the Anglo-American Club House, where I saw Negroes and whites drinking tea without spilling any on each other. The British Ministry of Information has set up several of these Anglo-American clubs, placing them in the hands of varying organizations. The club I visited is efficiently run by the Salvation Army. Another one that I know is run by Catholic sisters; another by the British Red Cross and St. John organization.

On the way home I asked the young woman driving my car and the attendant young man, a geologist working for the Ministry of Information, if they would stop at the church in Thaxted. It goes back to the fourteenth century. I wanted to look at the gargoyles and other carvings, some of them quite playful, on the exterior. We went inside. It seems to me I was never in another church so light and cheerful. Among the pictures and copies of pictures around its walls is a series depicting the four seasons. The one for spring, all bright and green, has this verse — quoted from I know not what poet — under it: —

> When every leaf is on its tree,
> When Robin's not a beggar,
> And Jenny Wren's a bride,
> And larks hang singing, singing, singing
> Over the wheat fields wide.

The picture and the words made me happy. I was not surprised to find hanging near by — in the children's part, I suppose — a picture in blue of Little Bo-Peep, with the old rhyme running back to the innocent days of long ago. They seemed now like an assurance and a benediction: —

Little Bo-Peep has lost her sheep
And cannot tell where to find them,
But leave them alone and they'll come home
And bring their tails behind them.

The bell-ringers were going in as we came out of the church, and presently the bells set up a most joyous ringing. Listening, I sat on the low churchyard wall and watched a string of carved sheep and dogs that have for all these centuries been frisking in stone over the wide church door. People with kind faces and clear eyes began entering for the services to which the bells were calling them. We had to leave. At least my hosts did; I wanted to linger there a long time. Across the street is an inn with the sign of The Swan painted, without words, in front of it. I should like to have a room in it and through its window look out on the sun-blest hills, at the saffron grain in the fields, and the young martins playing in the air, and listen to the joyous church bells.

As we rode away, the geologist told me a folk anecdote of two bishops who came into a great church. One said, "A place like this makes me feel little. I shrivel down until I am no bigger than a rat." The other said, "A place like this makes me expand until my soul seems to fill every corner and cranny."

CHAPTER XI
Coffee in Wales

THE ROAD to North Wales took me south to London. I had been there during several air raids, but on the night of March 24 I witnessed just about the climax of rocket gun action against the raiders. The only way I can suggest the sound of these rocket guns is to call upon all the "clatter wheels of hell," whatever they are, all of them, to clatter, rumble, thunder, roar, stampede, clash, rush headlong into each other and explode, filling the whole sky with their activity and adding their lights to those of enemy flares, search flares sent up from the ground, searchlights that come and go, assorted aerial explosions, with cloud reflections of blazing buildings. Horrible and terrible as the thing is, the spectacle and the sounds are dramatic beyond description.

The next morning my train left from the station it was due to leave from, though not on the accustomed track. I had stocked up on newspapers and magazines at one of the station stands, but traveling through a new country I always want to look and have no time for reading. The route was west by north — populated places, fields, sheep, always sheep, which in a moist country thicken the turf, rather than destroy it as in parts of the arid West. A fellow traveler called my attention to the Cotswolds as we passed through them — gracious hills with the most beautiful cottages in England. The English, high and low, rich and poor, educated and uneducated, all seem to love their lovely landscapes. I prefer to live in a country that is still developing, that has plenty of outlet, but for travel I'll choose a country with a past, with associations historical, literary, traditional, personal, attached to its places. Nothing is more vacant than a house that has never been lived in. . . . We crossed the Dee, "the sands of Dee," and were in North Wales. Before that I had seen the gorse in bloom. "Kissing will be out of fashion," they say, "when the gorse is out of bloom."

Foreigners are apt to think of Wales as a separate island. In places you can cross from England into Wales as imperceptibly as you can cross from North Dakota into South Dakota. It is the persistence of the Welsh people, who still speak Welsh, in addition to English, and have their own books and periodicals as well as traditions, that keeps Wales an integer in Great Britain. America has no monopoly on melting pots. I am a Borrovian, but not many people read George Borrow, who lived with the gipsies and wrote *Lavengro*, who fell in love with Isopel Berners and then out because she would not learn to read the fourteenth century Welsh bard Davydd ap Gwilym, who fancied horse-charmers, prize fighters, old applewomen and a mysterious man in black, who distributed Bibles and wrote the best book ever written about the Spanish people, *The Bible in Spain*, which was not translated into Spanish until the time of the late Spanish Republic and which is now characteristically banned by the Franco fascists. He wrote a book also entitled *Wild Wales*. I thought of it as the train twisted through the beautiful mountains, but they seemed less wild to me and are far more populated than the beautiful hills up the Colorado River in Texas.

My destination was Harlech on the sea, in sight of Snowdon, the most famous mountain south of Scotland. Before I got out of Wales I learned a lot about it from a recent book called *I Bought a Mountain*, written by a Canadian who acquired about three thousand areas of rough land in the Snowdon district and raised sheep; I really learned more about the Welsh "mountain sheep" than about the mountain. In Harlech the British Army Educational Corps has a college that gives a course every week to a class of Army and A.T.S. personnel. The college's invitation to the U.S. Army to send representatives has brought a few Americans. The idea is to give ideas and training in technique to discussion leaders in ABCA (Army Bureau of Current Affairs). My contribution was two talks about the U.S.A. I heard a few of the lectures but was more interested in the model conducted discussions on such subjects as Women after War, Sex Education, Postwar Homes, Wartime Marriages, Eire and War, What To Do with the Germans, Hong Kong, Canada's War Effort, France, British Agriculture, Schools, Use of Leisure, Social Security — subjects that are certainly "current." American officers in a position to know tell me that our army educational system is not nearly so well developed as the British. This, my own observations confirm. The American Army has had too many tabooed subjects, although it is becoming more realistic. Red Cross entertainment huts are a fine thing, but they do not make and will not save civilization. "Cultivated mind is the guardian of democracy."

I had time to explore by foot into the mountains. One afternoon I set out with Captain Davies and his wife, both Welsh. She had been an army nurse, had lost her health and had recovered it at a Welsh farm where we went. As the two-storied rock house, attached to about sixty acres of cultivatable land, is typical, I shall pause at it. When we arrived, the housewife and her daughter were sunning their pillows and cushions on a low stone fence. We went into the parlor and there on mantel and in cupboards I saw an extraordinary array of willow-pattern dishes and shining brass vessels and candlesticks. Soon we went into the combination kitchen and dining room for tea. Cured hog hams and sides of bacon hung from the massive and ancient beams holding up the low ceiling. The fireplace was big enough to hold a settle, but a wood cook-stove was fitted to one side of it. In one corner was an oak chest with "E. M. 1695" carved on it. Among crocks, one of them holding eggs, were more brass utensils. A shepherd dog stood with his head in the open outside door. Just beyond was a low stone dairy room. There was a radio, seldom played I was told. The house had its own electric plant. There was a great bounty of bread, butter, scones and cakes (not too sweet) with the tea. As lordly men, Captain Davies and I were served first.

He professed having business back at the college; his wife said he just did not want to walk. She and I "stepped on westward." The understanding, without obligation however, was that we would get back to Harleck for seven o'clock dinner. We kept walking along and through the rock fences that will remain for me the chief memory of Wales. Built generations ago, most of them are as good as ever they were and more beautiful, their lichened gray blending with the land as easily as a boulder washed by one of the mountain brooks. The skilled hands that constructed them were as harmonious with the earth as the slow forces of geology that made the rocks themselves. They carried me in imagination to the miles-long hacienda walls of rock going over the mountains in Mexico, and to Robert Frost. "Something there is that doesn't love a wall." Yet something there is that does love it. I met Mr. Frost while he was looking at rock fences in the hill country of Central Texas and was considering buying a farm there for the fence. "Good fences make good neighbors." I can find an abundance of black and white etchings and lithographs of Welsh castles, but I can't find a picture of a Welsh rock fence.

The road that Mrs. Davies and I walked got dimmer and dimmer. It would be impossible in that ancient country to get "beyond where the roads have been cut out." But we got beyond where automobiles make tracks. We came to the home place of a Welsh bard, Edmund Prys, who died in 1624. On Sundays in their chapels the Welsh people still sing his hymns in their own language. In a kind of cove on a mountainside, with a mill-wheel turned by waters of a little brook, we found the two-storied rock house, in excellent condition, nobody at home. I was glad of it. There are two good ways to look at antiquity: (1) with an informed guide, (2) without anybody at all to interfere with investigation and imagination. I paused at an old grindstone to sharpen the fine knife, with my name on its horn handle, that booted Harold Graves on the lovely San Bernard River near Brazoria, Texas, gave me years ago. I wished him there to turn the grindstone and witness my regard for the good steel. I looked through a notch between mountains up a valley and saw a little lake, shaggy black Welsh cattle on the far shore. The sudden appearance of a shepherd dog who said nothing indicated that somebody would return to the house after a while.

A man and a boy came. The man said his name was Jones — a very, very common name in Wales. He showed us inside. Again the quiet display on shelves and sideboards and in cabinets of blue willow-pattern china, burnished brass and copper, and some pewter. Upstairs in a bedroom very clean, he asked if we wanted to see "the bard's study." It was a mere clothes-closet in size. What had been the one window to it was walled up maybe two hundred years ago to escape the "window tax" then levied by the government — with the result that the rich turned several windows into a single bay-window, for the tax was on each window, regardless of size. I sat on the rock bench, built out as a part of the wall, that the bard used to sit on; there was just comfortable room in front of it for a small table no longer there. Outside again, I looked over the mountains and down on the lake and up the glen and through the trees and along the stone walls. Until that day I had never heard of the bard; I do not know a single word of his language; yet somehow I felt that I was understanding him.

It was now past seven o'clock. I had learned that walkers through Wales are accustomed to buying meals at any convenient farmhouse. I asked Jones what the chances were for getting supper at his place. He said that his house-keeper would be back "before long" and that she would provide us. He was a very tall man, a bachelor; he moved in a way to remind one of evening shadows; his voice was like a deep, strong shadow; it seemed to belong to the hills. While waiting for the housekeeper, Mrs. Davies and I stepped on still farther westward, up a glen that would be considered a good canyon back home. We got over a stone wall reinforced by barbed wire, though I doubt if it would stop any Welsh "mountain sheep" really wanting to get over. I saw a ram stand flat-footed and jump on top of a wall fully six feet high, then jump off on the other side. Everywhere we went there were young lambs "star-scatter'd on the grass." I had seen them all along the rail-road and was to see them again as far north as Edinburgh, as delightful as the "rathe primrose."

It was dusk when we got back to the bard's house. The housekeeper, agreeable of features but utterly uncom-municative, was about to prepare supper over a wood fire in a fireplace furnished with a fine iron crane to hang pots on. While we waited, I sat on a bench almost inside the fireplace itself. I remarked something to Mrs. Davies about four eggs being a good starter for a meal. The cook seemed interested. I told how Bigfoot Wallace once walked food-less two or three days to El Paso after the Indians had stolen his mules and at a Mexican house down the Rio Grande ate thirty-seven eggs and then made it on in, to a square meal. The cook said nothing, and Mr. Jones did not say anything either. I had noticed a crock of eggs.

The cook took down a side of bacon hanging from a beam and with a very sharp butcher knife sliced off some pieces. I wished her knife had not been so shaving-sharp; a dull knife cuts thick slices. She sliced from a loaf of brown bread about "as long as your arm" and four times thicker. Out in one of the rock barns, originally some sort of dwelling house, Jones had showed us the oven wherein this loaf was baked. The cook kept her back to me and was in such dim light that I could not detect the details of her operations. After a while, with one word only and a single gesture, she motioned us to seats at the table. She lit a kerosene lamp to add to the firelight. She brought two plates of food from the dimmed fireplace. In each was a solitary egg and two slices of bacon. The butter and bread, however, were unlimited and so was a jar of gooseberry jam, and there was an unstinted amount of milk to go with the tea. I never shall forgive myself for not saying something like this: "I will pay you whatever you ask for half a dozen fried eggs." I somehow had the idea that the eggs were rationed. The Welsh are very frugal and abstemious. I learned a little later, however, that neighborhood gossip does not ascribe total abstinence to Mr. Jones and his pleasant-featured but silent housekeeper. The two suppers cost four shillings (eighty cents).

Stars lighted the way back over the mountain. Country-bred Mrs. Davies led across and around fields, showing herself as good a guide as Bigfoot Wallace, even if she had had only one egg. A lone curlew cried from the sky.

A dog barked somewhere beyond a stone wall. An un-
identified bird sound made me think of a startled killdee.
After a while we came within hearing of guns practising
antitank fire. It was less than an hour till midnight when
we reached the college, where the military people were
having a dance to wind up their week's course. Captain
Davies was at the door. He said he had been worrying about
our not having supper.

I went back outside and from far below saw silhouetted
against the stars the towers of the castle built shortly after
William the Conqueror conquered England. While I was
at this place I saw them in sunshine, in mist, in dusk; from
above, from below. No other castle, unless it be the one at
Tours I saw in the last war, ever talked to me like this one.
One morning at the wall beyond the castle moat I lingered
a long time watching jackdaws building their nests
in the crannies of the towers and walls. These jackdaws make about the same sort of constant noises as
American jackdaws make and are about the same size, but
they have a slate-gray head. In nearly all the pictures of
old castles of Wales and Scotland jackdaws are in the air.
Looking at the birds while I talked to the porter who
helped with my bags at the railroad station, I spoke of their
cheerful talk. "That's nothing," he said, "to what they make
when each year a thousand Welsh people gather inside
the castle," which is roofless, "to sing their old songs and
hymns. While they sing, the jackdaws gather on the walls
by the hundreds and then they sing. Oh, it is beautiful and
wonderful to hear the people and the birds singing to each
other and together."

I told him that in my country the Mexican vaqueros and the coyotes sing that way to each other at night, each choir sending its voice to the stars. He told me that the name in Welsh for robin means "dear little robin."

I will not describe another long walk that I had up a vale, where gulls and blackbirds followed plows, and over more mountains, always within sight of gray rock fences and lambs. We came to where some farmers with shotguns were surrounding a few acres of forest and tangled undergrowth to get a shot at a fox that more farmers with terriers were trying to chase out. The fox had killed four lambs the night before. Earlier in the morning he had come close to one of the stands but the gunmen did not have their guns loaded and he got away before they could load. Hoping to see the fox, we stayed with these men of shotguns until they got tired of watching and straggled away.

I had to leave the trail to a bard's house, the green vale of gulls from the sea, the jackdaws dawing on castle walls, the beach where I walked by morning picking up shells and remembering other surf-beaten shores. Schoolteachers from all over Wales were gathering at the college in Bangor to hear knowledge and wisdom concerning the United Nations. The courses, popular over Britain, were initiated by the American Ambassador; O.W.I. had asked me to interpret the Constitution.

At Harlech you get tea before you are out of bed and tea for breakfast, but there is mid-morning coffee as well as after-dinner coffee. I left Harlech soon after breakfast and reached the college at Bangor, where a room was awaiting me, at lunch time. The college is up on a high hill an inconvenient distance from the town's center. Something was going on all afternoon; we had tea at teatime — and I looked forward to dinner coffee. We had tea; then I was pressed into leading a discussion and as a nightcap we had more tea. I thought to myself, "Well, this is one of those places where breakfast coffee is the rule for those who want it." At breakfast there wasn't any liquid but tea. I was told that there was no coffee on account of the scarcity of milk. You can't get around logic. Ireland is neutral on account of the presence of the Irish. In mid-morning I made my speech. Tea for lunch and then a busload of us went to visit a slate mine that was operating in Queen Elizabeth's time.

The Welsh teachers were lamenting over how vast dumps of slag cover fertile valley land under the mountain and mutilate the landscape. Talking with these teachers, I began to get a little into their feeling for nationality. They are proud of their own university, the Welsh National Museum at Cardiff, their national library, a Welsh magazine trying to revive Welsh literature, Welsh newspapers, the disestablishment of the Church in Wales, the perseverance of their own tongue, and Lloyd George. Some Welshmen dream of having a nation of their own, a member of the British Commonwealth of Nations. I think that they need to be penetrated by the English a good deal more than the English need to be penetrated by them. It is extraordinary how on this tight little island the two races have dwelt side by side for so long without blending more. Yet there are islands of Dutch, German and other nationalities in America that have kept their identity for generations, the youngest still speaking English with an accent that the Welsh do not generally show.

A slate-cutter at the mine allowed me to slice a square of slate. The work is far easier than splitting logs and a thousand times more pleasant than all day long screwing tap No. 422 on bolt No. 422A. And now it was the late afternoon of my second day without coffee. By the time we got back to the town of Bangor, my head felt as if the slate-cutter were exercising his craftsmanship on it. The teachers were hell-bent for a lecture on China. Alone I headed into a tiny, neat-looking tearoom.

"We don't serve coffee this time of day," the waitress said. Four young natives in uniform at a table had a hard time hiding their snigger. I walked out and down a canyon-like street until I came to the sign of a hotel. A cozy coal fire, quiet tables mostly vacant, low ceiling, brass platters dull on the wall against the kitchen, and the face of the one waitress told me I was in the right pew. I did not ask the waitress if she had coffee. "Young lady," I said, "I know you don't have any coffee made, but you can brew it, and you will be rewarded this side of heaven after you have brought it unto me. Furthermore, I will dance at your wedding with a cow bell on."

Without giving me time to grow impatient, she brought a whole pot, "hot as hell fire and strong as tobacco juice," with a small pitcher of hot milk to mix with it and hot buttered toast and jam. How blessed it is to receive, I thought. I swallowed as well as smelled. The kingdom of heaven was at hand and the meek were inheriting the earth. The mess of pottage that Esau made himself immortal by trading off his birthright for could not have been more delectable. Had I given that benison-bestowing damsel my bill-folder with all of the contents that a burglar stole out of another bill-folder, I should have but feebly, though only temporarily, have expressed the joy that came into me with the coffee. After the first half cup I stretched my legs and felt virtue going down into my toes. From mountain climbing I was footsore and leg-weary anyhow. I had taken a table hard by the fire; I had a fresh newspaper; I lingered and took mine ease in mine inn and considered what a good world this is. Whisky runs short, but I have not heard anybody ascribe the shortage to lack of water. When a man's whole system craves a certain kind of liquid, no substitute will suffice — unless he is perishing of thirst, and even then there are limits.

CHAPTER XII
There's Heather for Remembrance

WHEN THE Master of Emmanuel College at Cambridge, a border man himself, learned that I was going to spend a part of the Easter vacation in Cumberland on the Scottish border, he brought over thirteen books, eleven maps and one scrapbook out of his private collection for me to fortify myself with. As the old Spanish proverb has it, "He who would bring home the wealth of the Indies, must carry the wealth of the Indies with him." The Master was not very romantic about the Borderers of romance. "They were just a bunch of cow thieves and horse thieves," he said. To me, however, the desperate-riding "lifters" of long ago whose meat was fighting, whose proud words ring like spurs in the old ballads and whose passion was liberty — at least for themselves — are a world apart from skulking thieves of a neighbor's stock. I never understood these Borderers until I tried to understand the old Texas-Mexico bloody border, where Ewing Cameron and Mustang Gray gave the cowboys a reputation they have never lived down. Sir Walter Scott's *Rob Roy* remains the most revealing commentary on the Texas-Mexico border I have ever found. I read it young while I was living in the great Brush Country between the Nueces River and the Rio Grande. The ballads of raids, battles, mysteries and lovers' tragedies belonging to Rob Roy's border came later. Before I could read well myself, my father was reading *The Scottish Chiefs* aloud to us. Certainly, those chiefs were not thieves of any kind. Bruce and Wallace — old Bigfoot Wallace was descended from the clan — will be my heroes as long as I draw breath.

I

Shortly after I reached England, a lady in Cumberland wrote inviting me to pay a visit to her country home. Mrs. Mildred Thompson-Schwab by name, she was born in Texas and educated at Vassar College. Her husband, London born and a field artilleryman in the last war, has been a wealthy stockbroker in London. While their children were infants in the 'Twenties, they bought three pedigreed Guernsey cows, which they kept on a thirty-five-acre estate in southern England, in order to have clean, tuberculin-tested, nutritious milk for them. Meantime Captain Thompson-Schwab had acquired a shooting preserve of seven hundred acres, known as Kingfield and provided with a stately house, in the Cumberland hills, right against Scotland.

The land was mostly covered with rushes, cultivated fields of other days having been allowed to go back to Nature's waste. The three Guernsey cows, however, had given the captain such a positive relief from stocks and bonds, and a new calf had given him such unworldly delights, to be shared only by the mother cow herself, that he decided to reclaim Kingfield. In 1931 the family moved to it, still maintaining a home in London. The great blitz relieved them of the London house. Now six hundred of the seven hundred acres are properly drained and sown, growing mostly feed stuffs, and Captain Frank Thompson-Schwab is selling milk from a herd of Guernseys kept in scientifically-conducted stables and from another herd of pedigreed Ayrshire cows stabled on a sub-farm of the estate. He raises sheep, hogs and a few horses also.

I did not know all this when he met me at the train in a Ford station wagon, which he ordered from America before that type of car was on the English market. As we drove northward from Carlisle of ancient castle and cathedral and of houses wherein Sir Walter Scott married and Burns made verses, he pointed out Netherby Hall of the Graemes. In my day schoolboys all over faraway America knew Netherby as the place to which "brave young Lochinvar came out of the West" to rescue "fair Ellen" from "a laggard in love and a dastard in war," danced a measure with her, whispered in her ear, whisked her on his horse and was away with the whole Netherby clan after him. Oh,

> There was racing and chasing on Cannobie Lee,
> But the lost bride of Netherby ne'er did they see.

In a way it seemed as if I were coming home. All the way north as the land raised and population lessened, I seemed to be expanding and growing freer. At Kingfield, first thing, I had to greet the Guernsey cows, the Ayrshire

cows, the calves, two bulls, the yearling heifers, the Clydes-
dale horses, the lambing ewes, the peaches and grapes in
the hothouse, the gooseberry vines in the garden, the fine
variety of conifer trees in the yard, the cock pheasant ready
to dart through a hedge, a wild pigeon on the grass, the
little rabbits playing in a paddock, a blackbird singing from
a wire, a silent sawmill and a brook down the hill so soft
in its talk that it added to the peace.

Water runs everywhere in this rainy border country,
and all the soil, underlaid with clay, has to be drained. The
network of tile conduits, lines of them seven steps apart,
lies a little below plow-point level. Unless drained, even
steep hillsides grow little but rushes; drainage is necessary
for any nutritious grass. Raw land can be bought for a
few pounds per acre. It takes thirty pounds (one hundred
and twenty dollars) an acre to drain it properly. Some of
it has been drained for hundreds of years, but the drainage
has to be kept up. Millions of acres of English lands are
drained, upland as well as the fens. Hardly any other farm
worker is as important as the drainer. His knowledge of the
geography of the drain pipes and ditches is as wonderful as
old Jim Bridger's brain-maps of the Rocky Mountains. I
used to wonder why so many "ditch diggers" come into
English literature.

Free trade, which followed the industrialization of England and consequent exportation of manufactured goods,
brought disaster to agricultural prosperity. Now that the
country is again doing so well at feeding itself, postwar
policy of direct subsidies to agriculture, or of indirect subsidies through tariffs, is constantly discussed. British citizens

understand that tariffs are subsidies, and the open question is whether manufacturers or farmers are to be subsidized. Rabbits, like rushes, require no subsidies. At Kingfield some time ago, six hundred rabbits were killed in one drive; they are worth good money now, for the price of game meat is uncontrolled. It was a pair of these English rabbits turned loose in Australia that has cost that country millions. They multiplied faster than English sparrows in America.

My first breakfast at Kingfield was distinguished by two fresh eggs, as well as bacon. That morning some farm boys brought in plover (peewit, also peewee) eggs. The plovers were laying early, their nests crudely lined depressions in the earth; they were not yet setting. It is now against the law to sell plover eggs, but a single egg would on the black market of London bring maybe up to four "bob" (eighty cents). The Scottish drainer told me that when he was a boy he once found two hundred and fifty in a single day, selling them at sixpence (a dime) each. People don't eat larks or blackbirds or nightingales' tongues any more either. I found two plover nests of three eggs each. I will "hear about the graves of the martyrs the pee-wees crying" long after the void-filling sensation of their meaty eggs has been forgotten.

I was "finely suited" at Kingfield, but on the moors I could see the invisible tracks of the ancestors of the wild cattle of Chillingham that once roamed here; the wild cries of the unsettled curlews made me restless; across the dashing Liddisdale that separates England from Scotland I

had walked on a trail that I know Rob Roy, Johnnie Arm-
strong, doughty Douglas —

"My wound is deep, I fain would sleep" —

and many another brave Borderer once spurred over. Long
afterwards Sir Walter Scott rode this way in search of the
old ballads that his name will always be associated with. It
is said that Scott got the beat, the music, of his own brave
verse from the hoof-beats of his horse in the hills of the
Lowlands — as the walk of their horses around the sleeping herd at night gave the cowboy songmakers the slow
monotony of their bed-ground lullabies. I'd like to use for
a spittoon the skull of every radio jazz hound who scoots
"Oh, b-u-r-y me not on the l-o-n-e p-r-a-i-r-i-e" into a
skating rink whirl.

2

Kingfield by Liddisdale on the Scottish border was a
tonic, and the goodness of Mildred and Frank Thompson-
Schwab comes back to me now like the sound of a bell over
faraway water, but the plover's wailing cry was in my system and hoof-beats in my heart, even though I was afoot.
The train northward threaded through hills as barren as
Dead Horse Canyon. I thought it would be a fine thing
to get off at Melrose on the River Tweed and pass the
night in some old inn outside which Sir Walter used to

hitch his horse. I was forgetting the war. For days I had not heard a formation of war eagles. The host of the King's Arms assured me that I could not possibly get any kind of room in Melrose town. The military had everything. He advised me to go by bus to Galashiels three or four miles up the water. I went and at dark, after much walking and inquiring, found a cubby room, the last available, in the Thistle Hotel, two dollars for bed and breakfast. This is the standard price in modest establishments.

I was not to be turned off Sir Walter Scott's trail, however. The next day I rode a bus part way back to Melrose, descended, and walked two miles to Abbotsford. Several people had told me that I could not possibly get into it. A good-natured young soldier at the entrance to the grounds asked to see my identification card. I showed it to him and told him that I had come many thousands of miles to salute the memory of a great and good man who was my personal benefactor. He grinned and said to go on down to the house "and try."

At a door guarded by two sculptured staghounds I pulled a rod. Back in the big house a bell rang and a woman of dour countenance appeared. I was explaining to her when a man of eager countenance appeared. It did not take me long to decide that the man was the high court of justice. Three times he asserted that the place was closed to visitors, had been closed for three years, and was under military restriction. At each repetition his assertion was more relenting. I helped him relent.

I'll remember Sir Walter Scott's pocketknife. I consider that a respectable knife for a man should be big

enough to castrate a Spanish bull with; the Laird of Abbotsford's knife would have served on the bull of primordial
breed whose horns, among an array of antlers, hang in
Abbotsford Hall. I'll remember an old Scotch shield made
of bullhide; it made me think of Comanche shields of the
same stuff, particularly one that Charlie Goodnight and
his scouts cut into and as a lining between the hides found
the pages of Gibbon's *Decline and Fall of the Roman Empire*, and there in their camp on the Staked Plains, the
Goodnight scouts formed a literary circle, relaying the
separated pages to each other. As a picturer of riders and
fighters, Scott had to know about all sorts of arms and
other equipment; he loved the gear anyhow and assembled
a mass of it, just as Charles M. Russell assembled all sorts
of cowboy, Indian and other frontier gear for use in his
wonderful paintings. Charlie Russell loved all of his objects
too, and today anybody can see his collection in the studio
at Great Falls, Montana.

A third thing I'll remember about Abbotsford is the dining room overlooking the Tweed and the sweep of hills
beyond. It was here that they put Sir Walter's bed after
he had ridden his last ride. It was summertime. He looked
out on the beautiful water and on the heathered hills.
Lockhart, his son-in-law, wheeled him through the halls.
"I have seen much," he said, "but nothing like my ain
house." One morning some days later he sent for Lockhart. "Be a good man, my dear," he said and died. Lockhart's *Life of Scott* is one of the great biographies of the
world. I remember as if it were yesterday the circumstances under which I read it twenty-four years ago. Lock-

hart says that Scott was greater than anything he wrote. He was. He wasn't merely a writer; he was a man who wrote. Mark Twain was like him in being bigger and more interesting as a man than anything he wrote, and Albert Bigelow Paine's *Life of Mark Twain* is the only American biography of a writing man that remotely approaches Lockhart's Scott.

They hitched Sir Walter's horses to the hearse that carried his body to the beautiful ruins of Dryburgh Abbey on down the Tweed River. At a certain high place where Sir Walter always stopped to let his horses blow and to look at the wonderful view, the horses stopped again. I stopped there also. It was right that when Lockhart died they should have buried him at Sir Walter Scott's side.

Many men and many women have loved their country. I don't think any man ever loved the features of his country, its traditions, its songs, its heather and thistle, cottages and castles, waters and hills, braes and glens, the characteristics of its own people, its ghosts and its living blood more than Sir Walter Scott. He made his country more interesting, beautiful and dear for others, adding associations to and enriching a thousand items of the land. In memory few kings or presidents deserve the honor that is his.

From Abbotsford, I got to Melrose about one o'clock and went into the bar at The King's Arms for a glass of ale. In it I found four American flyers, a tall young man in Polish uniform, and a civilian. The civilian was playing darts with one of the airmen. Another airman was just about doing nothing. The other two were anything but moaning at the bar, where they stood gaily determined on demonstrating their generosity to any approacher. It would have been easier for me to drink water than pay for a Scotch. One of them spotted me as a Texan. They said they had got so thirsty on the train that they got off at Melrose, though they were headed for Edinburgh. That is where I was headed for also, with some more tramping in between and my traveling bag at Galashiels. I could have stayed at The King's Arms and been as matey as Tam O'Shanter with Soutter Johnnie, "o'er all the ills of life victorious." I lingered only long enough to miss a bus.

When I went out, the tall, fair-faced young man in Polish uniform went out also. I asked him about the chances of getting a taxi. He asked me to eat lunch with him. He said he was billeted in a house just around the corner and had his own meat, a big hunk of mutton he had bought on the quiet — illegally — from a farmer the day before. He said he wasn't any more Polish than I was, that he was Irish and had volunteered to join the Polish army because he wanted to fight for them and did not want to fight for the British. The mutton was vilely cooked. Young Ireland offered me an American cigarette out of a Lucky Strike package. "Black market," he explained, "and a God's blessing it is." He had been drinking whisky in the morning before the Americans arrived. He wanted to talk. He was against the Russians and against the British, against Mexico and for Franco. He did not mention the Germans. He was for the Poles, but seemed to be having a devil of a time making up his mind just whom to attack in order to battle for them. As we parted, he said he had to go and lay in a week's supply of whisky "from the black market." He is the first person in Britain that I have heard take pride in violating any law.

> If thou would'st view fair Melrose aright,
> Go visit it by the pale moonlight.

I could not do that. It was the wrong time of month. It would be useless to try to describe the ruined Abbey. Sir Walter Scott's descriptions have made it more beautiful. God is to be thanked that no Chamber of Commerce has backed restoration of it. The keeper showed me where the heart of Bruce, "petrified," is supposed to be buried. He gave me some sprigs of blooming heather, the white especially for luck, he said. I told him that my father's ancestors came from Scotland many generations ago and that I would send a sprig to my mother. I should not have been willing to leave the British Isles without seeing heather in bloom. "I do not think I could live without seeing heather at least once a year," Sir Walter Scott said. The sight of it made me realize keenly how much I love the mesquite, especially in its first greening. The keeper said he liked to read stories of Texas cowboys better than anything else.

He led me to the most famous gravestone in the churchyard. The inscription is but another example of how art is not what you say but the manner of saying it. It is but another example also — a supreme one — of the way in which man's imagination has in words, color, music and form made eloquent in multiplied versions the simple fact that the dust called man returns to dust: —

THE EARTH GOETH ON THE EARTH
GLISTERING LIKE GOLD.
THE EARTH GOES TO THE EARTH
SOONER THAN IT WOLD.
THE EARTH BUILDS ON THE EARTH
CASTLES AND TOWERS.
THE EARTH SAYS TO THE EARTH,
"ALL SHALL BE OURS."

3

At 8 P.M., I stood at the elevator door on the ground floor of a minor hotel on a side street in Edinburgh. The lay of the land indicated that the hotel office must be up-stairs, and there was no indication that the elevator would ever run again. Just as I decided to walk up, two American sergeants carrying pack kits breezed in and, with only a glance at me and the elevator stand, bolted for the stair-way. Two flights up, we found a handbell on a deserted desk. I rang it and put it down. One of the sergeants seized it and swung it as if he were Doomsday's commissar commissioned to wake the dead. All three of us had tried unsuccessfully at several hotels to find a vacant room. I asked the sergeants if they had been to the American Red Cross. "We're on leave to get away from soldiers," one said. Meanwhile a woman whose face indicated that she did not like being yelled at by a bell approached. She told me firmly that she did not have a single room. She conceded to the sergeants that she had a double room. I left them shelling out.

I knew I should not have to spend the night in a jail bed, as I have heard of travelers doing these congested days. The police, they say, will always take you in. In her home I had already found the volunteer secretary of the English-Speaking Union, which has no club rooms in Edinburgh, and she had offered to prepare me a bed in her own house. She told how a son of hers had experienced hospitality in America. A little later, weary of the search, I telephoned her. She had located a room in a modest private hotel, which I found run by a hearty woman and her brother. I'll long remember the sandwiches this good woman prepared for the train trip when I left three days later and how she and her brother stood in the door and waved and waved at me as I drove off in a taxicab.

The second evening in Edinburgh I had dinner with another pair of kind hearts, an eminent doctor and his wife. When I left, they asked me to direct some American soldier to their home. Some old men are dull because they have never got over being born that way; some are interesting because their minds are stored with observations and experiences; a few are wise from a power to make just deductions from a lifetime's massing of evidence. Doctor Sinclair is one of the wisest men, as well as one of the finest gentlemen, I have ever talked with. He said that in watching the careers of many men he had come to the conclusion that energy and the application of it count more for accomplishment than mere ability, though energy, of course, must have a requisite amount of ability to work with.

THERE'S HEATHER FOR REMEMBRANCE   233

I had spent the whole day looking at the great Edinburgh Castle, Holyrood, with Queen Mary's "secret staircase" to her lover's chamber, and other sights for sightseers. None of these fine things talked to me like a fife and fiddle that two street musicians were playing on my way to the doctor's home. I don't know what they were playing. It was some tune of the Scots folk, old and plain, such as "the weavers in the sun do use to chant." I lingered a little to listen to it and to contribute my sixpence. I wished I had no other engagement but to follow them around. The tune took me back to one night in Oklahoma City twenty years ago when I heard a blind woman, accompanied by a freckle-faced, snaggle-toothed girl holding a tin cup for coins, singing "When Work's All Done This Fall" and playing the tune on her guitar. I persuaded her to sing it three times, and many a time since the melody she made of that old cowboy song has come back to me. It will be thus with the tune of the fifer and the fiddler in a street of Edinburgh. It seemed to me to express

> Some natural sorrow, loss or pain
> That has been, and may be again.
> The music in my heart I bore
> Long after it was heard no more.

It made me remember, too, an old crippled man with drooping mustaches, whose looks, corroborated by answers to questions, showed he had once ridden free over the range, that I came upon hunkered down with his fiddle against the wall in a sunshiny spot on Houston Street in San Antonio one winter morning a long time ago. I asked him to play "Hell among the Yearlings," and he played it and "Rye Whiskey" and "The Gal I Left Behind Me" and one or two other pieces before I left. Well, blessings on all street singers and players! I had far rather encounter one than a skyscraper or a motor ramp, a mayor or a staff colonel with a staff car and a head full of important exclusive information. I wish I could go to Ireland and find the Fiddler of Dooney.

> When I play on my fiddle in Dooney,
> Folk dance like a wave of the sea.

In London, walking on a quiet street, I once stopped to listen to a barrel organ and talk with the organist. He told me how two American soldiers had intercepted a policeman trying to "interfere" with him; how he had bought the organ for thirty pounds and was keeping himself in "clean clothes" and in food with it; how he had the prospect of some more tunes, secondhand of course, for none are manufactured now, to grind out; and how occasionally he got "a bit of silver" as well as copper. A woman gave him a bit just as I was moving off. It's a long way to Tipperary — but no place is far from Tipperary, or Red River Shore, My Old Kentucky Home, Greenland's Icy Mountains or India's Coral Strand when the tune is right.

The tune was right all the time in Edinburgh. I have not seen many of the great cities of the world, but I must think that none of them has anything fairer than Princes Street. It is wide and clean and runs alongside a deep and wide glen. The houses are built on one side only of Princes Street, the other side, next to the glen, being open so that

people can look down on the grass and trees and across it
to the castle walls and towers on a craggy promontory and
then at the "royal mile" of ancient High Street stretching
from castle to Queen Mary's Holyrood.

The tonic air and the "look and a half away" here gave me
a kind of expanding feeling I always have when I get west
of the Pecos. The feeling had additions to it when in the
morning I walked through the roomy Botanical Gardens
of Edinburgh. They run up on an outlook over Firth and
hills, north and south; they run down to a pond of little
lowlands. A part of them are planted with many varieties
of heather, and the heather was in bloom. So were rhodo-
dendrons and clouds of yellow daffodils on the slopes. The
blackbirds were singing blithe. The few people about all
looked kin to the green grass and the heather. Something
in me wanted to sing with the birds. Every tree, shrub,
bulb and flower in these gardens is tagged by name so that
a visitor may add knowledge to sensory impressions.

I was delighted to find Robert Louis Stevenson's child-
hood home, preserved as a memorial, just across the street
from the Botanical Gardens. Pictures, letters and other
things therein brought back to my memory many a good
deed his writings have done to me. There was the late night
in a boarding house, upstairs, about December of the year
1910, when, reading *Treasure Island* and hearing in imagination sinister John Silver's pegleg tapping the floor, I was
startled almost out of my skin by a noise in the hall. It was
actually a sheet of newspaper blown along the floor by the
opening blast of the first hard norther, coming "sudden
and soon," of the season. I imagine that not many readers

have heard John Silver's stump, stump, stump so real-
istically. In this Stevenson home I learned that the bronze
medallion of him made by Saint-Gaudens is in Saint Giles
Cathedral. Many times I have looked at pictures of that
reclining figure and longed to see the original. I went
straightway across town and amid all the memorials on the
cathedral walls found it. A very large part of Stevenson's
forty-four years of life was a gallant fight against disease,
during which he was always tugging at the skirts of the
old world and calling it to come and play. Saint-Gaudens
has him sitting up eager in a bed, Stevenson's own words
graved by it: —

> Youth now flies on feathered feet. . . .
> Where hath fleeting beauty led?
> To the doorway of the dead.
> Life is over, life was gay:
> We have come the primrose way.

But the church authorities directed substitution of one of
Stevenson's Prayers for the primrose words.

On the longish trip home I observed afresh the extraordinary ability that some people, both English and American,
have for sleeping and being bored, or perhaps, as they sit
with lackluster eye gazing at a wall instead of out, only
blank. We pulled into Cambridge just as the sun was setting
red and a squadron of planes flew across it on lowering
way to their bed grounds. During sixteen days to the west
and in the north country I had missed them acutely, roar-
ing over day and night, morning and evening, in shining
dawn, in blind darkness: the formations of destiny, flying,

always flying, seldom so many coming back as go out, yet their volume ever increasing.

Among letters awaiting me was one enclosing a clipping on the death of Colonel John W. Thomason of the United States Marine Corps, author of *Fix Bayonets*, *Jeb Stuart* and *Lone Star Preacher*. I had carried with me, with the intention of answering it, though I did not get to it, a letter that must have been among the last he wrote. "The Empire's impact on you gives me no concern," he wrote, "for I am also a fairly wide-traveled Texican. Cities and dreams and Powers simply remind us of something better than we know ourselves. . . . When this is over, I shall return to Texas, and I look forward to seeing you there."

Well, I had looked forward also. I imagined a cool place in the shade along in the evening, with perhaps something else cooling befitting the time of day, and talk until long after dusk had blurred the shadows. I imagined Paul Wakefield and John McGinnis there, two men that John Thomason liked and that admire him. Now we won't ever sit in the shadow made by a great elm tree, but the gracious shadow that his imagination cast upon the land of his birth will never be entirely blurred out. In these accounts of my own little excursions into Wales and Scotland I have spoken of men who by their art have enriched the features of their land, adding to them memories, pictures, incidents, interpretations, making them more delightful and ennobling for all mankind.

To this company of enrichers John W. Thomason surely belongs. In the person of Praxitiles Swan, the "Lone Star Preacher," and his comrades, all the memories of the Texas men in gray are gathered up. They are saturated with whatever it is that the pines and the prairies of their soil infuse into human nature and with a belief in "something" that will make their lost, and perhaps wrong, cause forever noble.

"For those men believed in something. They counted life a light thing to lay down in the faith they bore. They were terrible in battle. They were generous in victory. They rose from defeat to fight again, and while they lived they were formidable. There were not enough of them; that is all."

It has been seriously said that Sir Walter Scott's romances were responsible for Southern conceptions of chivalry and thus for the Civil War. However that may be, those "long-boned, hairy fellows" of the South were "in their simplicity, their earnestness and their antique courage," and in the desperate firmness of their belief in "something," the counterpart of

> Scots wha hae wi' Wallace bled,
> Scots, wham Bruce has aften led . . .

John W. Thomason's realization, without sermonizing insistence, of this belief makes his book for me the most moving and the most heart-lightening piece of writing that, so far as I have read, the Civil War has inspired. I record a personal impression, not a criticism. It would be a reassuring thing if one could feel that the millions in khaki in these years of Part Two of the World Wars so assuredly "believed in something."

CHAPTER XIII
"I Always Did Like Harmony"

I CAN'T REMEMBER a time before I heard my mother describe someone — not always complimentarily — as "grinning like a Cheshire cat." The Cheshire Cat, you know, "vanished quite slowly, beginning with the end of its tail and ending with the grin, which remained some time after the rest of it had gone." I went to Cheshire (the county, in northward England) hoping to see one of the cats. Nobody that I talked to had ever seen the grin, and if they have not seen the grin, naturally they have not seen the cat that grins. Cheshire cheese is in these wartimes about as rare.

Nearly all the country houses and also town houses in England are named — in the manner of ranches and office buildings at home. On the edge of a little village in the hills occupied by an American military outfit, I stayed at Orchard Lea. It is well-named, for the house, modern in design, is set in a ramifying garden that runs into an orchard, and the orchard runs into a meadow of about fifty acres, joined by other meadows and fields. In the yard, against the lane, or road, is a magnificent beech tree that has been declared a national monument. It is safe from

axe and saw, though many fine groves throughout the
country have been commandeered for timber.

My host was a man past sixty-five years of age who
served as infantry colonel in the last war. He manufactures
a form of ammunition that the Germans have learned about.
His wife, a strong marshaler of affairs, works as hard with
her vegetables, flowers and chickens as any farmer, but
she had two maids to keep the extensive house and help
make it a refuge for Americans.

The colonel represents a type of Englishman by no means
obsolete. He has never let business atrophy the art of living. He reads for another reason than to kill time, has com-
piled a local history, draws, wood-carves — some of his
handiwork being on the house — has collected a fine library of natural history and sporting books, has hunted
and fished in many places, does not like at all the government trend towards socialization but realizes that a short-
range, small-caliber charlatan in politics cannot effect a
long-range, big-gauge policy. The walls of the home are
lined with pictures of landscapes, animals both wild and
domestic, birds, flowers, human nature, historical places.
I thought of a certain big house with many bathrooms built
by a rancher whose sole decorations in his ample den con-
sist of multiplied enlargements of Kodak pictures of himself and his prize Hereford bulls. The colonel told me that
he rents his meadowland, the turf of which has not been
plowed up for sixty years, at the equivalent of nine dollars
per acre. The land itself might be worth three hundred dollars per acre. After taxes, upkeep of fences, and so on, are

taken out, the net income is about one per cent. Britishers with surplus capital have been and still are salting away their money in land, with the result that income on it is very low and that nobody could borrow money, buy land and make a living on it. I saw about thirty-five head of cows and two-year-old heifers grazing on the meadows, the grass so good that they were filled up and lying down by ten o'clock in the morning. Some of the cows were branded with a small circle on the right horn. As a rule, however, nobody brands cattle at all in this country.

In a U. S. Army jeep provided for my benefit, we rode into moorlands that seemed as high and waste as the Highlands of Scotland. At one place where butts have been built as stands for grouse shooters, we got out and walked and lingered. We started up two or three grouse and could hear them calling in every direction. We saw snipe flying and could hear them drumming on the descent. The lapwing was flying and calling its lonely cry. The "wandering voice" of a cuckoo went up a valley. I felt far away and free. The sheep on these moors are the largest I have ever seen anywhere; they have the look and movement of primitive animals.

Motionless in a hedge near Orchard Lea, I watched a pair of partridges that did not see me but that were never a second not on the alert — quiveringly alert — against enemies. The male was calling his mating call loud and high, but when he moved across the grass he ran towards cover and ran very low. When he put up his head to look, he was in tall grass. One day when the wind was from the east, my hostess led me to a wren's nest in a plum tree; the wren's head was towards the east. The next day the wind was raw out of the north; the little sitting wren had her head to the north. For fifteen minutes I watched and listened to a thrush sing without a stop. He sat on a small, down-hanging limb of a horse chestnut white with flowers. He has the variety but lacks the energy and delirium of our mockingbird. I like the old name "throstle" better than "thrush." "And hark, how blithe the throstle sings!" But is not mockingbird a flat, too literal, name? I wish we had adopted the Indian name, zenzontle, used by the Mexicans for it, as we have adopted mesquite, coyote, huisache and many another native name for native life.

While we were in the garden — and during daylight hours I never stayed in the house — we saw a wood pigeon, the bird that steals most from farmers, that is most persecuted and yet seems to thrive everywhere. For me, the calls of the bob white and field lark have more cheerful peace in them than any other bird sounds, but many people would agree with John Cowper Powys that the wood pigeon's "murmur is the most soothing of all sounds on earth." My hostess asked if I knew what the wood pigeons say. One coos to the planter, "Sow more peas, sow more peas." Its mate joins in, "Do, do." Again it says, "Ours is a nice house, ours is." According to another translation, it says, "Buy two cows, Sammie, buy two cows." In another part of the country it goes, "Take two, Taffy, take two." This is not very complimentary to Taffy, which is the name to which David, by way of Welsh *Tavid* (Dafydd), long ago descended.

> Taffy was a Welshman, Taffy was a thief,
> Taffy came to our house and stole a piece of beef.

That is not just to Taffy's character, but the wood pigeon does not know anything about the matter. Sometimes it says, "I love Bertha, I love Bertha." I told my instructress in pigeon English how the dove talks in Mexican: "*Que quieres, pastor, que quieres?*" "*Comer comas, comer comas.*" ("What do you wish, shepherd, what do you wish?" "To eat coma berries, to eat coma berries.")

We saw a magpie. "Take your hat off to it," the colonel said. That is to avoid bad luck. "One for sorrow," the old rhyme goes —

> One for sorrow,
> Two for mirth,
> Three for a wedding,
> Four for a birth,
> Five for silver,
> Six for gold,
> Seven's a tale that's never been told.

The rhyme varies, like all old spoken things living through human memories and voices and not petrified into print. It takes you back to quiet days of long ago —

> Five for a fiddle,
> Six for a dance,
> Seven for England,
> Eight for France —

And this may have been chanted to magpies in the days of Joan of Arc.

There's a yellowhammer on top of the hawthorn hedge. All through the summer he'll keep on singing, "Little bit of bread and no cheese."

The colonel told me about a man he knew whose horse fell, permanently crippling the rider, right after this rider had seen a single magpie without taking his hat off to it. He never again neglected to observe the hat-to-magpie formality. It is notable how people not generally superstitious take stock in some particular superstition. In England, as in many other parts of the world, the swallow is regarded as a harbinger of good fortune and to destroy a swallow's nest is to invite ill fortune. All day long the swallows dip about Orchard Lea, their flight always bringing to my mind the waltz strains of "*La Golondrina*," which means "The Swallow" and which is certainly the translation of motion into sound. Not long after the owners of Orchard Lea came to occupy it, the mistress of the house destroyed a nest built at a place whence the swallows interfered with human cleanliness. Very soon thereafter she had to undergo a series of operations. The colonel still feels that destroying the nest had something to do with the matter.

Without being what one would call superstitious, he senses mysteries beyond philosophy. He does not believe, however, that a buck deer can translate itself into a hare. And yet — one time up in the Highlands, he and his stalker, having located by telescope a stag and five hinds, spent a long time crawling up for a shot. The wind was with them, and cover was excellent. When they raised up about a hundred and forty yards from the deer, the hinds were moving off. "Deer will move that way sometimes without having sensed anything directly." They counted the hinds, one, two, three, four, five. The stag should have been following them. "He habitually follows." But the stag was not following the hinds. He was nowhere in sight. He could not have got away in any other direction than that the hinds were taking. He had simply disappeared in a manner altogether unaccountable. On the exact spot of ground where he had been, a solitary hare now squatted. The stalker said, "They say a stag does that sometimes." Another stalker, to whom the colonel later related the experience, asked, "Did you shoot at the hare?" "No." As Matthew Arnold said, "Explanations are always tedious." Without going into explanations, the stalker indicated that it is never judicious to shoot, or even to shoot at, a hare into which a stag has turned himself.

I told the colonel how some of Pancho Villa's men believed that he could, and in hard places did, change himself into a black stallion that would run riderless across a battle-field, too swift for any rifleman to hit. Of course, the black stallion would later turn back into Villa. No Villista ever saw the transformation. They would see Pancho Villa; a minute later they could not see him but would be gazing at the black stallion. A Villa veteran in Parral, Chihuahua, told me that in one battle Villa's horse was shot dead under him, and that while the enemy, already almost on the leader, came on, Villa disappeared. The veteran had information that, in this tight place, Pancho Villa turned himself into an ant and crawled under the horse.

The colonel and his wife have a home in South Wales.

Some Welsh people near them, much disturbed by a ghost, persuaded a curate of the Established Church of England to lay it. He drove a stake through a leg of mutton, pinning it to the bottom of a brook, and recited appropriate words in Latin. The Welsh were ever mystics. They say that the best bull-tamer is an idiot boy. The bull will walk up to him and ask to have his head scratched.

My hosts are not race-horse people, though they like races. They told of a noted jockey of times not long past. He had lost a leg and would go limping along, up and down, on his peg. He was dried up and wore a battered hat. He generally wore an old dirty raincoat half in shreds. He looked like something the rats had discarded, but all the horsemen sought his opinions on horses; owners contended to get him to ride their racers, and bettors followed him more than the horses with their bets.

This jockey made me remember J. R. Williams's cartoon of "The Rusty King" in *Out Our Way*. I have admired its trueness to range life dozens of times. There on an old sleepy-eyed, flop-lipped mare, her draggletail matted with cockleburs, wearing a blind bridle, the reins to which are a piece of calf rope, the cattle king sits in a kid's saddle with stirrups a foot too short. From the way his eyes are squinted, though, you know he's sizing up every pound of flesh on the cow brutes he's inspecting. And Curley — ah what a piece of reality Curley is! — says, "He told me his secret of success was that every time he saved enough money to look like a cowboy's supposed to look, he'd buy another ranch."

In front of the fire, we talked about many things, from

the way Mexican vaqueros break horses to chaffinch eggs.
They told how a modern English servant will describe
callers. "There's an elderly person to see you, sir." (A
woman, maybe a charwoman, maybe a "half lady," maybe
just "a cup of tea.") "There's a young person to see you,
sir." (A young woman.) "There's a man to see you sir."
(A man of whatever degree.) "There's an individual to
see you, sir." (Anybody with an axe to grind, a gold
brick to sell, a crank religion to expound, a pittance to beg.)

I do not think, however, that pretense words are as far
advanced among the English as among Americans. By
"pretense words" I mean words used to disguise reality.
In America we started out with "graveyard," got up to
"cemetery," and now have graduated to "memorial park,"
though, whatever you call it, the place is a place for
shoveling corpses under the ground. So also in America
the undertakers now palm themselves off as "morticians,"
the only difference between an undertaker and a mortician
being that the latter charges more for an imitation grass
carpet at the grave and other glass-bead disguises of the
very necessary but unloved business of burying dead
people. "Earth to earth," and letting the petals of a rose
fall on the coffin instead of a bit of genuine dirt, does not
diminish the smell of mortality. Other pretense words not
yet advanced to radio use in England are "message" and
"special announcement" when nothing but a damned advertisement is to follow. In other words, the English have
not got so far along in lying to themselves or in paying
mountebanks to lie to them.

It is good to leave a place while you wish you could

linger. On the ways to and from Cheshire, I saw the countryside at its best, in early May. I wonder what it was
like five hundred, a thousand years ago — say in the savage
times of King Alfred. I am sure it was not so gracious as
it is now, with flowering trees introduced from abroad,
with little gardens everywhere belonging to homes that fit
into the earth. English people have made the English land
more gracious; it, in turn, has made them more gracious.

On the way home on the train I fell to talking with an
American sergeant who joined the army under Pershing
on the Mexican border in 1917, who has been in it ever
since, and who had arrived in England from Alaska only
a few weeks back. While we were looking out the window
at the green and pleasant land, cows grazing on the grass,
hawthorn hedges bursting into white, red and white tulips
banked against a brick cottage mellowed by the weather
of many summers and winters, he said: "I hope I'll get
so I can understand these English people, but look — I
always did like harmony."

CHAPTER XIV
At The Anchor

THERE ARE numerous pubs in Cambridge — The Baron of Beef, out of bounds for American soldiers; The Angel, where soldiers are too thick for anybody else to get in bounds; The Castle, where the matured barmaid combines dignity with easy welcome; The Jug and Bottle, where citizens take their pitchers to be filled; The Red Cow, too cavelike for cheer; The Bun Shop, often in stock when other pubs have run out but too garrulous for conversation; The Hat and Feathers, too far away; The Little Rose, just what it should be. But after I found my place at The Anchor, I always felt I was missing something good in life if I went anywhere else. It is at the foot of Silver Street by a bridge and over a fall in the Cam River.

The time I began finding it a refuge was when darkness came early and black curtains shut off the view from the river, but the ingle fire was "bleezing finely." Then the days lengthened, and from the seat by the window that I always seemed to find — by being prompt at the six o'clock opening — I could see the mallard duck with her little ones, which grew up and practised skimming. In the elm trees beyond the river and a bit of fen, the rooks talked about their nests, their eggs, their young ones and other things until they all went away. A contented white cow seemed to spend the summer lying down on the patch of fen grass, where a moor hen walked with her solitary hatchling. It was a sight when in September the pair of white swans that use far up the river came around the bend convoying their eight half-grown grayish cygnets, the male in the lead and the female guarding the rear, the whole line moving as stately as a formation of cruisers. Unless the weather is atrocious, lads and lassies are always in punts rowing and poling. How beautiful the water dripping from oars is in the slant sunshine! A boy is always fishing from the bridge; I have never seen his patience interrupted by a fish.

Jack Barrett, the proprietor of The Anchor, rents boats from his little wharf. After the beer shortage forced him to start opening an hour late, he allowed a half-dozen of us to go in the back way daily at the accustomed hour, draw our own bitter and sit down in an upper room — against the river always. One evening when I came in, I met him and an American soldier alone at the bar. The soldier was drinking barley water flavored with lemon. He never drinks anything strong, he said.

"How did you get in the back way?" I asked him.

"Why, he's my boy," Jack Barrett explained. "He always comes here for a boat when he gets to Cambridge. He goes down the river alone, way past the locks and on. We took to each other as soon as I met him."

"Yes," the soldier from California went on, "this is my home when I can get off. I stay here. I wrote back home that there's somebody over here I call 'Mother.' "

"I told him," said Jack, "that he could describe her as

my bed-mate." Then he added, "I'd adopt him if I could."

Jack is a philosopher, kind of partridge-built, quick as a cat on his feet, light always dancing in his eyes. I don't know anybody more cheerful than he and his wife are. She draws beer as steadily and expeditiously as he does. "I been to a place where I saw a little motto framed on the wall," Jack went on, talking to me and the California soldier. "I was afraid I might forget it and I copied it down. I needn't though, for it's in me mind. It says, 'Make yourself at home. Home is where you can grumble.'"

"At home," I said, "an American thinks heaven is where he ain't, and when he's somewhere else besides home he thinks heaven is what he's used to."

"That's all right," Jack said. "When I was a young fellow like him here, I knew a man that didn't stay home very reg'lar. One day I says to him, 'Can you look me in the eye and say you have never broken your marriage vows?' 'Jack,' he says, 'I ain't never exactly broke 'em, but I've sure give 'em a hell of a twist sometimes.'"

"There was one of your English poets named Ernest Dowson," I added, "who wrote a poem to some woman. I don't know whether she was his wife or not, probably not."

"Probably not," Jack agreed.

"Anyway, at the end of each verse he said, 'I've been true to you in my fashion.'"

"Well, it's all in definitions," Jack concluded.

He and his helpmate have for years kept The Anchor clean and cozy, making a good living, I suppose, adding to human sanity and cheer I know. If they operated such an establishment in America, they'd take in a barrel of money. They'd enlarge it to take care of more and more customers and keep on enlarging it until it grew as big as Madison Square Garden, or else became a standardized unit in a standardized chain. Long before reaching either stage, however, it would have lost the character that makes the snug little public houses and inns of England veritable "islands of the blest."

The good English publican is certainly not averse to making money, but he is content with making a living. His pub has likely been a pub for generations without appreciable growth. The pictures on its walls go back sometimes as far as the walls themselves. They are quiet, inclining to landscapes, coaches, cheerful faces, hounds, horses, foxes, horsemen, all sorts of sporting subjects — except sporting women. This is the very opposite of the American bar pictures, which are designed to inflame all the lusts. The absence of silence-murdering noises from radios, nickelodeons and slot machines harmonizes with the pictures. In all the pubs you can play darts free. The proprietor is not trying to peddle sidelines — and calling his peddling "service." The gin mills of British cities have been very different institutions from the modest pubs I have in mind.

These pubs do not try to make drinking "attractive." Ideally, they are just homy spots among a very settled and not at all Bohemian population. They are more cheerful than merry. Before the next authority polishes off his final chapter on "The Phlegmatic English," he should harbor in a few of them.

I and my cronies at The Anchor gravitate to our table without any priorities. Horner went to sea at the age of thirteen, made a stake in Venezuela oil, knows the oil fields of Persia, Texas and Mexico; says the only reason he is not a millionaire is that he has never really known but two kinds of people — seamen and gentlemen; lards his talk often with Spanish words. His tongue is bitter against many things — women, because they spend their lives making men think that unessential things, like furniture, napkins, sheets and silver plate, are essential; politicians, the Prime Minister included, because they compromise even liberty and tax the taxable in order to effect their compromises; civic filthiness, as evidenced by the dog-dung spattered on streets, seldom cleaned in wartime; the blasted superficiality and bogus pretense of education resulting from popularization of it. Horner's tongue is so sharp, so withering, so fiery that I wonder he can generate saliva at all. Yet his heart is mellow. He drinks only one pint of ale. To hear him talk, you would suppose that as soon as the war is over he is going to the head of the Amazon River and live naked in a jungle where the accursed hypocrises and idiocies of purported civilization will not fret his Timon-like sensibilities. He reads, but I have never heard him quote George Bernard Shaw; he needs no scripture for his anathemas.

Biglow is of a serene nature. He was wounded twice in the air in the last war. He does Red Cross work now, smokes a pipe continually, laughing at the tax on tobacco, drinks three or four pints between puffs. He is always agreeable. Back in the days of Pancho Villa, before the last war, he was a young blade in Mexico, mining and helping a syndicate promote a mine at Mazapil that he now inclines to think fulfilled Mark Twain's definition of a mine: A hole in the ground and a liar on top. It turns out that he and I have ridden the same trails in the Sierra Madre. I knew the old British Vice-Consul at Durango when he was drinking about a quart of tequila a day — equal in potency to maybe two quarts of whisky — and held the record for having killed a wild turkey gobbler that weighed forty pounds. Biglow knew him when Pancho Villa came to Durango and demanded 20,000 pesos from the British consulate, whereupon this Vice-Consul, representing all the Americans left in the city as well as his own nationals, called on Villa, told him that the British Government did not allow any money for ransoms, and ended up by taking 20,000 pesos for charity distribution that Villa had just printed in the form of streetcar tokens.

Biglow remembers how charming the señoritas on the plaza looked at night with the lightning bugs in their hair. He passed a note to one of them and with encouragement "played bear" at her window — but the bars were a terrible impediment. He and I get to remembering and drop into Mexican phrases and laugh and in imagination get us a couple of *músicos* and sit down at a table on the plaza to be serenaded while we eat double-fried frijoles. What a lot of pleasant places and hearty ways of life and genial people there are in this world to experience and then remember!

The major, a medico, belongs to a Highland regiment two hundred and fifty years old. He says that the first

Highlanders to discard kilts were young men who attended the University of Edinburgh and that the discarding was to signify they had been educated. He says that the only two proper uses of the word "Scotch" are in "Scotch whisky" and "Scotch oats." It is not proper to speak of a Scotchman; call him a Scot or a Scotsman. His remedy for colds is of Cornish origin: Hang a boot over foot of bed; go to bed; drink whisky till you see two boots; go to sleep.

Put back into civilian life after the Burma campaign, the Doctor has charge of the blood-transfusion business for a large region. His soft voice and winsome manner always melt me. We were talking about Henry VIII. Horner said that when Henry VIII was young, he was truly noble; that he was ruined by Anne Boleyn, who had her head cut off properly. I wanted the Doctor's opinion on a matter about the great marrying King that I heard from a Londoner replete with underground history. This Londoner said that Henry contracted syphilis and that the doctors prescribed virgins as a cure or palliative. Hence the succession of young wives. The Doctor replied that ignorant people, especially in the country, still think contact with a virgin may cure a man of lesser venereal diseases. He said that wigs came into style because some Lord who had lost his hair on account of syphilis set the fashion, to cover up his baldness.

Somebody asked me if wigs are not worn by judges in America. I replied no, that Thomas Jefferson's comparison of a man's head under a wig to a rat under a pile of old dirty clothes influenced the first national justices to eschew them. I must say that I have seen nothing that suggests senility with more emphasis than a wig on an old man in a chair of state. Another fashion, that of high collars for women, was set, Horner said, by Queen Alexandra, in order to disguise an excrescence on her neck.

This talk about queens prompted the young Director of Public Works to pull out of his pocket a list of Assyrian names for girls. The prettiest name, I thought, was one meaning Dew. The word *dew* is not in itself beautiful — like *dusky*, say — but all of its connotations are fresh and fair.

I asked the Doctor about those natives of Kenya who drain blood out of living cattle to drink, along with milk. He said that owing to drought there are about two months in the year when the cattle don't have blood or milk either, and that then the nomads have to go on a vegetable diet, principally wheat; that it upsets their digestive systems and they are very unhappy. The enforced demand for wheat has resulted in a few men's turning from the pastoral life to an agricultural one, but the nomadic cattle owners look upon the planters with contempt. I grew up, I said, on the same sort of occupational distinction, the old *puro ranchero* type calling farmers "clodhoppers," "cotton-backs," "hoe men," and generally regarding them with about as much admiration as the spurred knight-at-arms regarded yon varlet "louted low down on his knee." Of course the stock-farming combination has changed this.

The Doctor told how Burmese priests are embalmed in honey when they die. "You are careful about eating honey in Burma," he said. That reminded Biglow of how Mexi-

cans embalmed the three-hundred-pound body of Boss
Shepherd in lime at the old Batopilas mines in Chihuahua
and carried the box out over the mule trail afoot, twelve
peons to the shift.

One day the genial authority on Estonia, jellied eel and
animal migrations gave us a mild toast: —

> Here's to your blood and here's to your health.
> If your blood's not good, your health can't be good.
> So here's to your bloody health.

The word "bloody" never fails to strike conversation
from an Englishman. Of course it no longer carries the
odium that made a Victorian mother ban it as one of two
unutterable expressions for her daughter. (She didn't know
any others herself.) Horner said that "blasted" became
popular as a substitute for "bloody," just as "darn" arose
to take the place of "damn." He cited the case of a man
who tried to recover damages for having been called a
"bloody scoundrel." The judge ruled that there was no
cause for damages but declared that had the defendant
called the accuser a "scoundrel," without the adjective,
there would have been cause. In other words, "When you
call me that name, smile," and "bloody" was the smile. I
asked the table if they had heard General Eisenhower's
judgment. They hadn't.

An American colonel in General Ike's Allied staff
called another colonel a "British son-of-a-bitch." The
breach of harmony came to the General's attention and he
ordered the American colonel to explain. After listening,
he announced, "I'll admit that you had grounds for irrita-

tion. Had you just called him a son-of-a-bitch, I'd over-look the matter. But you called him a 'British son-of-a-bitch.' You are relieved of duty here and ordered back to Washington."

This brought up the case of "the intrusive *h*." According-ing to correspondence in *The Times*, as "the Anchorites" recalled, a hundred years ago or so upper-class Englishmen frequently dropped their *h*'s where they shouldn't and intruded them just as the uncultivated do today. Rather recently a newspaper critic in reviewing the singing of a young Englishman noted that "a keen ear can detect the intrusive *h* in certain words of his songs." The singer sued for damages — and recovered.

These are just samples of our pub talk. I sit on my "throne of human felicity," as Doctor Johnson defined a tavern chair, in The Anchor and remember the conclu-sion that old John Adams made to a famous passage he wrote on the "balancing" forces in the American Con-stitution. "All this complication of constitutional machin-ery," he said, "all those wheels within wheels, have not been sufficient to satisfy the people. They have invented a balance to all balances in their caucuses. We have con-gressional caucuses, state caucuses, county caucuses, town caucuses, parish caucuses, and Sunday caucuses at church doors; and in these aristocratical caucuses elections are decided." The English pub is not only "the poor man's club," as it is often called; it is the common man's caucus. If I were a Gallup poll inquisitor, I should not want a better test tube for analyzing what's in the English wind than the English pubs.

Not that politics afford by any means the chief theme of conversation. The British admire much more than they exclaim. An American "pub crawler," a sort of lone wolf who frequents where army uniforms are scarce, tells me that admiration for General Patton's daring and speed became for a while the chief theme over English pint measures. The patrons of a country pub will spend an evening speculating on how partridges mate, for no man, they say, has ever seen the mating. Natural history will abide as a subject long after opinions of what to do with the Germans have become obsolete. It may abide longer than the combine harvester, but probably not longer than the annual prospect for the wheat crop.

Neither ale nor beer — they are the same thing — taken moderately is highly potent as "conversation juice." I have watched a laborer sip at his pint for an hour without saying a word, just sitting and thinking or maybe just sitting. These days you never know what is running in the mind of a man old enough to be the father of a soldier boy or girl. I have seen a whole table of slow drinkers, drinking as slow as a cloud drifts in a windless sky, sit in such silence that I recalled the night Charles Lamb, walking home with a convivial companion, stuck his head in a window where glum company sat and shouted out, "All silent and all damned." Nevertheless, the pub is English fellowship.

I never go anywhere in England without noting the names of the pubs. They make a kind of poem. Many of the signs are still pictures, sometimes without the words appropriate to them, sometimes with. The White Horse and

The White Hart, for instance, are likely to have nothing but the pictures. The Jericho House sign (in Oxford) has under it the scriptural legend: "And the King said, 'Tarry at Jericho until your beards be grown.'" Labour in Vain shows two women trying to scrub the color out of a Negro. The Honest Lawyer pictures a man carrying his head under his arm; The Silent Woman has her head in the same position.

A proprietor would not think of changing an old name in order to advertise his own. The mellowness of the old is loved. The proprietor of The Cock (in the Lake District) learned that change might lead to something approaching ruin. A bishop moved into the vicinity of The Cock, and out of compliment to him this proprietor renamed his place The Bishop and had a sign painter paint a mitered head on the board. There was a rival house across the road, not well patronized, and as soon as the progressive proprietor of The Cock discarded that sign, his hungry rival appropriated it, discarding the one that had failed to attract. The new sign drew customers like flies, drew them away from The Bishop. The ecclesiastical dignitary, who had felt flattered by the compliment, passed by not long after it had been made and saw in large letters under what was supposed to be his head these words: THIS IS THE OLD COCK.

The George and Dragon recurs frequently. One day a tramp-looking man stepped into an inn bearing this sign and asked the woman behind the bar for a drink of water. She was bothered and cross that day, which is not at all the habitual way of barmaids of any age. "We don't give drink to tramps," she scowled. "Get gone." He got, but within two or three minutes put his head back into the open door. The barmaid of The George and Dragon saw him and called, "Well, what is it this time?" "I was just looking to see if George might be anywheres about," he answered.

The Vicar of Wakefield, in Bedford, has a benevolent exterior. I suppose The Pilgrim's Progress is to be found somewhere in that town. Slow and Easy, The Bank of Friendship, The Travellers' Rest, The Good Companion, Live and Let Live, The Jolly Miller, The Jolly Farmer, The Old English Gentleman, The Barley Mow, The Five Bells, The Eight Bells, The Golden Hind, The Pike and Eel, The Pack Horse, The Hammer and The Anvil, The Swan with Two Necks, The Dog and Pheasant, The Hounds and Fox, The Wild Boar, The Cherry Tree, The Four Ashes, The Fox and Grapes, The Cottage of Comfort, The Cat and Fiddle — all these and many another have made me wish that I could stop — aye, linger — at each of them and inhale its flavor. The flavor of life they all assuredly have. "Well," as the fellow says in the play, "here's to temperance."

CHAPTER XV
What England Did to Me

THE FINAL CHAPTER to this book that I wrote in England would not fit. Now, back in America, I am writing something that, whether it fits or not, must be in a different key and must have a different tone. I write in an atmosphere as remote from the air of intellectual freedom enveloping Cambridge as was the atmosphere over "the wild New England shore" when the Pilgrims moored their bark upon it. I write from a plot of ground, delightful in itself, against the campus of the University of Texas, in Austin. Here on this campus, believers in the right as well as the duty to think are combating a gang of fascist-minded regents: oil millionaires, corporation lawyers, a lobbyist and a medical politician, who in anachronistic rage against liberal thought malign all liberals as "communists," try with physical power to wall out ideas, and resort to chicanery as sickening as it is cheap. My mind is paralyzed by this manifestation of "the American way of life."

I

Sailing west from the British Isles, I cabined with an English civilian who told me this about himself: "I am sixty-one years old. I was born and reared in Pennsylvania. My parents were German, with a touch of Irish. I grew up in an atmosphere hostile to the English. In 1914, at the age of thirty-one, I went to England, spent a night in London in the old Morley Hotel on Trafalgar Square, and when I woke up in the morning realized that for the first time in my life I was at home. I have lived in England, never far from London, ever since."

I understood him. The impact of England was gradual upon my own consciousness. I have known, in broken spells, harmony with my own environments the greater part of my life. I have known it best when I was doing the kind of work I wanted to do in the way I wanted to do it; I have known it with individual human beings; I have known it with nature — more jubilantly perhaps in the vast and unpeopled mountains of western Mexico than anywhere else. Before I went to England I never knew any consistent harmony with what is called "civilization" —American civilization as it is realized in cities, expressed in newspapers, blared out over the radio, and otherwise proclaimed. I have never felt harmony with that civilization as it tries to flower, but generally balls, in American universities. Now, however, that the humanities are cutting loose from the German Ph.D. strait jacket, they may

enjoy some freedom. To find harmony, I have had to flee
the stridencies, not the strenuousness, the insincerities and
blatancies of much that passes for Americanism. The ways
of life that I have been in harmony with in my own country have not been typical of the vaunted "American way."

Many times I have thought that the greatest happiness
possible to a man — probably not to a woman — is to become civilized, to know the pageant of the past, to love
the beautiful, to have just ideas of values and proportions,
and then, retaining his animal spirits and appetites, to live
in a wilderness where nature is congenial, with a few
barbarians to afford picturesqueness and human relations.
The young Englishman Frederick Ruxton camping in the
Rocky Mountains a hundred years ago with his pack mules,
his Pancho horse and a lobo wolf, now and then seeing
trappers and Taos Mexicans, while guarding his scalp
from Indians, satisfies this ideal. According to it, civilization is necessary to give a man perspective; but is otherwise either a mere substitute for primitiveness or else a
background to flee from.

Such an ideal was never practicable except to a few
individuals who in retreating from society substituted
camp fire for ivory tower. In this shrinking world, it
becomes less and less practicable. It precludes the idea of a
civilized democracy — though any democracy will be
tolerant of nonconformists who draw off to one side as
well as of those who march in the ranks.

Some thoughtful Englishmen fear lest civilization, accepting the popular American conception of civilization,
will destroy their culture. By culture here I mean not only

traditions but traditional outlook derived from the cultivation of mind, body and spirit. American culture is derived largely from frontier life, from space. Population,
wealth, mechanical comforts and luxuries and urban living
have already largely destroyed that frontier culture. Among
tens of millions of Americans, civilization has come to mean
the diffusion of manufactured contrivances. The disciplines
that created old civilizations have certainly been in retreat against the advance of machine civilization. Machine
civilization has not yet had time to demonstrate whether it
can create a culture that gives graciousness, charm, depth
and tolerance to human life.

In England I was for the first time in my life really confined to civilization — in the old sense of the word. Barring
some inconveniences, I liked it. If at times I grew hungry
for spaces, I readily found that cultivated nature gave me
freedom and joy. Life in an old English college is subject
to certain formulas. Yet that life came to me to seem
freer of rigidities than much American life, either in or
out of a college. This sense of at-easeness, of freedom, is
hard for me to explain. Perhaps it depends on the presence
of a tolerance made modest by centuries of custom. I
believe that it depends also on the absence of propaganda
and other forms of controls that big business in America
has come to exercise or to try to exercise on all mediums
of expression — an unannounced but pervasive fascism,
reaching down into primers for infants and up into popular
magazines too holy to accept advertisements. The absence
of sinister designs, like the absence of noise, contributes
to peace of mind.

At any rate, while England gave me serenity and a sense of freedom, it gave me a more critical attitude towards life. I suppose this is a concomitant of civilization. Matthew Arnold defined poetry as "criticism of life."

Under bombs both piloted and pilotless I have felt more serene than I can feel under the everlasting bombing by American avarice wanting to sell me not only goods but a dependence upon goods and calling its business "service," seeking to hinder the spread of truth and the play of ideas and calling its conduct "free enterprise." It is no wonder that young Americans, especially young soldiers, have become as distrustful of the motives behind truth as they are of the motives behind axe-grinders. Little in their training, either pre-military or military, has conduced to the process of clear thinking. Their "opiate" has been not the religion of a church but that of the National Association of Manufacturers. When their distrust brings to them more confusion than enlightenment, it serves their manipulators as well as ignorant trust serves.

"The trail is counter, you false Danish dogs," who restrict your fear of regimentation to government bureaus. We Americans have a promoted mass movement for loving our mothers — promoted by the sellers of gifts; another mass promotion for appreciation of dads, and yet another for remembering the dead. We have proclamations for clean-up week, for garden-planting week, for go-to-church week, for cutting-ragweeds week, for careful-driving week, and proclaiming governors with the brains of adding machines alone know how many other special weeks. Not alone our physical acts but our ethics and our very emotions are to be channeled, standardized, mass-formulated.

England, even among its crowded millions receiving war as well as making it, renewed in me a feeling for the individual. I go to a football game at home, and while I hear and look at the organized cheering, I remember the casualness with which a crowd in bleachers viewed a game of rugby between Oxford and Cambridge teams. Each of the loosely massed spectators seemed to feel as easy with himself as if he were fishing alone on a sunlit riverbank. The crowd applauded good plays on either side — without orders from any cheer leader to goose-step.

England gave me a fresh realization of proportions. At the American football game I have just spoken of, two bands paraded the field between halves — a truly colorful spectacle; but each played two local college tunes at which the crowds were expected to rise and stand with as much reverence as if the national anthem were being played. I like to stand for the national anthem; the music and the standing both make me proud and give me noble feelings and bring long memories. Every time one goes through the motions of saluting a bed sheet, the dignity of the salute to the country's flag is lowered.

One early morning I was in a Red Cross Club at a bomber base in East Anglia where I had talked the night before. The only people in it were the Red Cross woman, three or four servants scrubbing the floors and washing dishes, and a big, good-natured sergeant from Oregon. He wouldn't dance, the Red Cross woman charged him, but she thanked him for always helping decorate for the dances.

Presently he said, "Before the thundering herd comes in I'm going to practise at the piano." He spoke of how it would be possible to keep the British Broadcasting Corporation radio on all day without being driven mad by the advertisements and the "murder of silence" palmed off on the public as music. He said that a good many soldiers had come to prefer British news broadcasts because they are generally more direct than the American broadcasts, which often "seem to be trying to sell the news as well as something that the sponsor of the broadcast has to sell." He wondered whether the American people really want to be constantly "sold" on something. He said that he could make a clock strike twelve times every hour but that noon would still come only once a day and midnight only once between sunset and dawn, yet the radio people often try to make the clock strike twelve even on the quarter hours.

He might have added that if he listened to the B. B. C. clear around the clock he would be unable to hear a syllable from some brass-lined, steel-headed, metal-voiced, hollow-tile-hearted, data-manufacturing, conclusion-prefabricated commentator. In the name of free speech and free enterprise, Americans will stand more propaganda than any other people outside of Russia and Germany. A great many of them have sense enough to be impervious to it. It is probably good taste as much as good sense that saves the British from such sluices of not only sterile but fertility-choking lava.

2

"He valued 'suffrages' at a most low figure," Carlyle said of his boyhood schoolmaster, a Scot. Few Englishmen have the "you-be-damned sort of attitude" of one of Kipling's characters, but their national motto is not "We Aim to Please." "The Irish and the Welsh are difficult people for the English and the Scotch to know or to understand," says Margot Asquith in her wise little book *Off the Record*. "Their desire to please — though a loveable desire — does not commend itself to candid and simple people. You either please or you do not please; in any case, it is not of paramount importance."

It is of paramount importance that a person be candid, be what he is. Contrasting the two countries, Henry Steele Commager said that political democracy is farther advanced in England and social democracy in America. In agreeing, I would add that the working of social democracy in America has made an enormous number of Americans expend an enormous amount of energy and endure an enormous amount of uneasiness within themselves, subjecting themselves to constant financial strain, in order to keep up with the Joneses. More than once I have been embarrassed in England by the apology of some American sergeant or other enlisted man for not being an officer. I remember in particular a gunner whose chief contribution to the conversation at dinner was explaining how at his bomber base he did not have to salute officers. You would have to go a long way to find an English or a Scotch noncommissioned officer apologizing for his rank. In the realm of naturalness a solid red cow does not apologize for not having a white face.

The English belong in the realm of naturalness. I doubt if between the sexes one tenth as much effort is exerted by one sex to impress the other as in America. America has never coined an Americanism more expressive of the country's modern spirit than the special use of "sell" in such phrases as "sell himself," "sold on the idea," and so on. The average Englishman would shrink from the idea of selling himself; on the other hand, because you do not want to buy the article, he will not discount it a penny.

It is pleasant to dwell in the realm of naturalness. George Borrow did not want to wash in a basin inside the house. "I am a primitive sort of man," he said to Jenny at the pump, and doused his head under the stream that she pumped. Too much has, I think, been said of English bluntness. You will during one day in New York encounter more harshness — from elevator operators in public buildings, bus conductors, keepers of newsstands and other folk — than during a whole year in London. After a sojourn in wartime regimented England, Americans upon returning to these democratic shores note the incivilities of civil servants. The natural courtesy and unaffected kindness of the English made a far deeper impression on me than traditional bluntness.

"The way to get along with the British," a much-traveled friend counseled as I was leaving for England, "is to tell them to go to hell." I found no occasion for that procedure. The way to get along with the British is their own way of getting along with each other: Be yourself. The "go to hell" attitude is a holdover from the age that prompted James Russell Lowell to write (1869) "On a Certain Condescension in Foreigners." "It will," he said, "take England a great while to get over her airs of patronage toward us, or even passably to conceal them."

I doubt if any people can conceal "airs of patronage." An English attempt, on a national scale, to practise deception would be as ridiculous as Malvolio's assumption of the courtier's smile and cross-gartered yellow stockings. The fact is that the English in general have gotten over their patronizing ways. In *The American Language*, Mr. H. L. Mencken — himself probably America's largest contributor among sneerers — amasses all the evidence of colonial and succeeding times to show British contempt for and patronization of American diversions from the King's English. What George III's court said about the independence of the United States of America would represent current British respect for this mighty nation about as well as most of the Mencken evidence represents the modern British attitude. In British eyes America is full grown. The English do not relish domination by American economic power, but they have in their realistic way accepted the fact. They prefer their own slang to American slang; yet they constantly adopt vigorous, picturesque American expressions. They consider that they have a right to pronounce their own language in their own way. No newspaper, magazine or individual in their realm has become distinguished for being anti-American. They are in a position where they have to play second fiddle to America in many ways, but — considering anti-British feeling and talk among Americans — their tolerance and dignity are astounding. No, they are not shaking "that rattle" in American faces any longer. Of course, there are always exceptions to any rule. A few Southerners are still fighting the Civil War.

3

The leaders of a country may or may not be typical; when they are ample, they are representative. Lincoln was not typical of lawyers or of the citizens who elected him; he was vastly representative, compassing in himself many types and individuals. Harding was merely typical. The English have a way of electing to their government men more representative than typical. Individuals often drop out of the so-called "governing class"; individuals enter it from other classes. The "class" maintains itself only by virtue of the fact that the people composing it are trained in the science of government, are competent, and are responsible. One would have to read far into Hansard's full reports of Parliamentary debates to find an example of the moronic puerility exemplified in the *Congressional Record* almost daily. The English educational system is not equalitarian in the manner of the American system; it does not recognize every boy as a possible prime minister; yet it certainly does train leaders.

The Evening News recently printed a protest against a move on the part of London cabmen to elect one of their number to Parliament to represent cabby interests. A Member of the House of Commons, the protester pointed out, should be larger than a "delegate sent by a sectional interest to plug that interest." In America we are used to two kinds of lobbyists; one paid by special interests to work on Congress and legislatures from the outside, and one elected — largely by special interests — to work inside. Parliament may have a few such members; they are not in the tradition of the British government.

Such legislators might at times be useful in performing limited governmental functions. They could never lead a government. They could never advance the civilization of a country and contribute to its culture. Yet the tradition of English statesmanship is the tradition of advancers of civilization and of contributors to culture. The amplitude of Churchill's nature, the prodigality of his wit and the compass of his imagination are hardly realized in his paintings or in his fiction, but they are suggested. Disraeli's epigrams may keep his name alive longer than his career as prime minister. Macaulay's work as historian and man of letters have already overshadowed his useful Parliamentary career. It was Burke's great mind operating in conversation, not in his sublime eloquence, that "called forth" all of Doctor Johnson's powers. The many-sidedness of Thomas Jefferson sets him increasingly apart from traditional American statesmen. Theodore Roosevelt has been the only president who might have written a book like Viscount Grey of Fallodon's *The Charm of Birds* — the

kind of book one expects from the ranks of English statesmen.

Emerson observed in Walter Savage Landor "a wonderful brain, despotic, violent and inexhaustible, meant for a
soldier, by what chance converted to letters; in which
there is not a style nor a tint not known to him, yet with
an English appetite for action and heroes." Byron was, in
effect, a warrior; Shakespeare managed a theater. The
soldier and man of action, Field Marshal Wavell, whose
brilliant accomplishments in Africa, achieved with such
slender means, were built upon by General Montgomery
and the Allied armies, brings out with commentaries of pith
an anthology of memorized poetry entitled *Other Men's
Flowers*. Lawrence of Arabia translated action into spirit-
riven prose. In or out of government, this mixture of the
elements in Englishmen is constant. Whether it is owing to
something racial, to long-absorbed Greek ideal of balance,
to both, or to other elements, I do not know. I know that it
both reflects and engenders richness of life. It is civilized.

It is the very antipodes of the powerful and persistent
American doctrine that businessmen should run the government, also education, and that a poet like Archibald
MacLeish is to be distrusted even in a minor government
post. William Randolph Hearst buys art in wholesale lots,
but somehow he has never melted the beautiful and the
free into his own soul. The people running the British
government have for centuries stood steadfast on the idea
that government should secure capital; they have not been
capitalists themselves, though many of them have been
men of capital. They have never confused humanism with

unfitness for active life, or liberalism with anarchy. John Locke, who died two hundred and forty years ago, perhaps best formulated the idea that it is the function of government to secure property. He had an immense influence on Jefferson, but when Jefferson nominated the unalienable rights of man to "life, liberty and the pursuit of happiness," he emphatically omitted *property*. In the Warren G. Harding prayer for "more business in government" flowered Jacksonian democracy's denial of the Jefferson idea of a civilization fostering liberal thought and humanism. The stark passion for stark business in charge of government will have nothing to do with the thinking and imagining class. Nor have the thinkers and imaginers of America compounded much action within themselves. No country has ever had more of idealism in government, but idealism flows in one stream and materialism in another, not confluently. The businessman's government, instead of adding sweetness and warmth and grace to national life, making it more fluid, has added barrenness and constricted it. This, even while democratizing material prosperity and manufactured goods.

It takes the human race a long time to adjust itself to revolutionary physical changes; the World Wars might be traced to the Industrial Revolution inaugurated a century and a half ago. It usually takes even longer for revolutionary thoughts to work home. Charles Darwin published *The Origin of Species* in 1859. Before that civilized man could look — historically — for perfection only in the receding past. There had been a paradise on earth, in the Garden of Eden — though the earth was very sparsely populated at the time. Profane historians conspired with biblical to place the ideal life far back, beyond recall.

> Then none was for a party;
>   Then all were for the State;
> Then the great man helped the poor,
>   And the poor man loved the great;
> Then lands were fairly portioned;
>   Then spoils were fairly sold;
> The Romans were like brothers
>   In the brave days of old.

The theory of evolution implied, in Darwin's own words, a belief that "man in the distant future will be a far more perfect creature than he now is, . . . after long-continued slow progress." At first common men regarded this theory, if they regarded it at all, with hostility, because it apparently contradicted something in their religion. Even after the theory became commonly accepted, it was accepted merely as theory, only remotely connected with man's daily life on earth. At last, however, the import of evolution is coming home. Better ways of living lie ahead, not behind. By taking thought, by employing science in its widest meaning, man can add more than one cubit unto his stature.

Few Englishmen, rich or poor, expect to go back to normalcy. Normalcy was ugly, like the word. Normal life ahead comprises something beyond what electrical fixtures can supply. The economy of the nation did not just happen. Man brought it about. Man can manage it so as to benefit from it in a more democratic way. Yet management does not imply a Russian break with the long continuity of English tradition. To find hope, English people need not migrate to a new world. They have the intelligence and the power to renew their own world. In other words, the British, the conservative English especially, have comprehended the meaning of evolution.

This deduction did not come to me from reading Parliamentary debates, though some debates on the Education bill, the Beveridge Plan and other subjects warrant it. It did not define itself to me anywhere in the multitudinous plans for rebuilding demolished cities and better utilizing the lovely country; yet many plans imply it. I probably base it more on the facts and enthusiasms encountered in youth conferences all over the land and on the spirit of promoting and receiving ABCA (Army Bureau of Current Affairs) among the young men and young women of the British armed forces. The air in England is not static.

4

Thought is the weariest of all the Titans. Love has many times been explained away; I doubt if ever once it has been explained in. I did not come to like the English because of expositions about them. My liking must have sprung from English literature — and in the long run nothing else so represents the life and spirit of a people as their literature. There is no literature apart from imagination and the emotions. English people on their own good land and in their own mutilated cities were increasingly, so long as I dwelt among them, personifying for me English literature. In a way not intended by the paradoxer, nature followed art.

In a British port I stood on the deck of a lighter carrying many young English wives of American soldiers to the great ship soon to take them to unknown homes. The solemnity of saying good-by, perhaps forever, to their native soil and the wonder, with something of fear, of what might lie ahead were deep in their eyes and on the strained features of their faces. One very young wife said to me, in her low voice, "I know something about American men. I am married to one. This baby is his as well as mine. But I do not understand American women. I have never talked to them. Their voices seem so loud." Voices from a group of young American women on deck pierced the air. Surely the culture, or control, of vitality does not wither it. All sounds of nature — the source of vitality — give a normal human being feelings of harmony. A panther's squall is a lullaby compared with woman shrillness. I recall often the soothing nature in voices of certain American women. I think that modern party-going has intensified the stridency of many feminine voices in America. At constant parties and conventions they raise and raise their voices to be heard over other voices. I cannot conceive of a more alarming sound than the blend coming out of a big room full of talking American women.

"Their voices seem so loud," the young English wife of the American soldier said, very low. Then, all at once, the representative tone of the voices of Englishwomen came to me, "She left an echo in the sense." But before I heard

voices of Englishwomen in their native land, I knew, without particular realization, of their quality. Now on the deck
of the lighter, what I knew came really home. Standing over
dead Cordelia's body, the wheel at last having "come full
circle" for him, spent King Lear said — and it was the last
fine truth of life he spoke: —

> Her voice was ever soft,
> Gentle, and low, an excellent thing in woman.

Twenty years ago on the plaza in Santa Fe I bought an
earthen jar from a Pueblo Indian woman. I bought it because it made me feel pleasant. It has a bird painted on it.
After I had paid the woman her dollar, just at which time
her husband came up, I asked her what bird the picture
represents. She looked at the bird, she looked at her benign-
featured husband, she looked at me, and then with a laugh
that rippled into the sunshine she said, "*Es un pájaro que
canta*" — "It is a bird that sings." I don't believe that any
ornithologist, or any anthropologist either, could give the
Latin name for that bird. But the Pueblo Indian was dead
right, and likely she didn't know why.

It is a long way from Santa Fe plaza to a plane tree in a
college garden in Cambridge, to Dartmouth House on
Charles Street in London, to a certain cheer-lit home down
in Suffolk — to forty dozen particular English places that
gleam in my memory. The one thing that I really know
about England is that it made whatever it is that is inside
me respond in the manner of the bird on the Pueblo jar.

THE END

Index

Date Due